Why People Do Bad Things

in the Name of Religion

Why People Do Bad Things

in the Name of Religion

by
Richard E. Wentz

• Mercer •

ISBN 0-86554-431-X   MUP/H344

Why People Do Bad Things in the Name of Religion
Copyright ©1993
Mercer University Press, Macon, Georgia 31207
All rights reserved
Printed in the United States of America

The paper used in this publication meets the minimum requirements
of American National Standard for Information Sciences—
Permanence of Paper for Printed Library Materials,
ANSI Z39.48–1984.

Library of Congress Cataloging-in-Publication Data
Wentz, Richard E.
Why people do bad things in the name of religion /
by Richard E. Wentz.
vii+106pp. 6x9" (15x22cm.).
Rev. ed. of : Why do people do bad things
in the name of religion? c1987.
ISBN 0-86554-431-X.
1. Religions.   2. Fanaticism.   3. Violence—Religious aspects.
4. Religious tolerance.   5. Humility—Religious aspects.
I. Wentz, Richard E. Why do people do bad things
in the name of religion? II. Title.
BL85.W44   1993
291.1'72—dc20   93-32630
                                        CIP

Contents

For
Nam Key-Young

A man of peace
who smiles with a Buddha-smile

Across the silent waters
The moon passes in a haze—
Noodles and tea.

Foreword

This is a book about violence done in the name of religion. It is a personal statement, a personal essay. There are many books that can and should be written to address this age-old issue. Although I am a historian of religion accustomed to the methods of the social sciences as well as the humanities, I have chosen not to write a critical, academic study. I have tried to share my insights, derived from the study of religion, in a personal manner. The sociologist is interested in religion as a form of *sociality*, of society and social reality. As a scholar of religion I use sociology in order to understand religion, but, in contrast to many sociologists, I understand society and sociality as manifestations of human religiousness.

The reader will certainly become aware that social, economic, and political factors must be considered in any discussion of the violence that is done in the name of religion. It will be discovered that the religious pursuit of ultimate order and meaning expresses itself socially, economically, and politically. Our political and economic needs will often determine the manner in which we use our religions. Certainly our religious inclinations will express themselves economically, politically, and even scientifically.

My statement stands as a single and direct contribution to the discussion. I trust it may lead many readers into further study, I offer it because I believe that it is necessary to begin this discussion with a question that attempts to reach as many thinking people as possible. It is deplorable to me that scholars of religion speak only to each other about issues that are close to the hearts of all of us. If this book leads someone to open his mind to the need for understanding religion, if it leads a single scholar to take to his own desk in order to correct my oversights, then my writing has not been in vain.

—*Richard E. Wentz*

Raising the Question

I am a child of the twentieth century, observing the waning years of this century. I have watched the television screen and read the daily newspaper with fear, indignation, and anger. How is it possible, I constantly ask myself, for people to be so convinced of the righteousness of their causes that they justify murder and the burning and destruction of home and temple? I know why that is so and I know that religion is not at fault. People are at fault, and their religions often tell us why.

It is said that Aśoka, that great Buddhist emperor of India in the third century B.C.C, publicly renounced his ways of violence when he became a follower of Buddha. It was painful for him to think of his earlier acts of carnage. He repented and declared he would never again draw his sword for purposes of conquest. He wished all living beings nonviolence, self-control, and the practice of serenity and compassion. Tradition says that no neighboring ruler ever took advantage of Aśoka's piety and compassion to attack him militarily. Perhaps it is also true, as Buddhist lore would have it, that this is the only example in human history of a major conqueror renouncing war and violence, yet remaining a benign and successful leader. Nevertheless, it is also true that we may find many Christians, Jews, and humanists who live by the spirit of love and compassion. And there are Muslims for whom jihad means only the discipline that is necessary to follow the path of God that Muhammad has revealed. They do not cry, "In the name of God, the Compassionate, the Almighty," then string up an alleged Israeli collaborator in Sidon's main square while a crowd chants, "Go to hell."

The question we face is, Why do *some* people often do bad things in the name of religion, while others do mostly good things in the name of religion? An understanding of religion helps to answer this question. Without such understanding, I have no genuine means of overcoming my own anxiety about this matter.

Henry David Thoreau wondered how it could be that "the humble life of a jewish peasant should have force to make a New York bishop so bigoted." I have wondered as much, and so have you. How can the ideas of any one human being be so important that they make us angry at others? Is anyone so important? How can I become so loyal to the person and work of a teacher of right living that I decide to do hurtful things to those who respect a different teacher? Or, what if we both claim we are followers of the same teacher, the same teachings, yet disagree with each other so violently that we do each other harm?

I once sat in the living room of a friend. We were having after-dinner coffee. Three of us were guests in the home of this benign gentleman, a retired rancher from North Dakota. He was a lover of the arts, a peaceful man, but when he invited the three of us to his home for dinner, he had not reckoned with the covert violence of his designs. Among the three guests was a professor of philosophy, whom life had treated rather shabbily. All this I was to learn later. He had an Irish name and a bad temper. He had been brought up a Roman Catholic—an Irish Catholic. Something had turned him very sour on his Catholicism, and his subsequent life as a philosopher had provided him with a battlement from which he could fire away at the least sign of religious intruders. He was a very logical person. He was also relentless, a bit ruthless.

My wife and I were introduced to him. Who was I? A new professor at the university having come to inaugurate a religious studies program. A historian of religion. The philosopher heard only the word "religion"; he began to train his guns. Religion was the source, the cause, of most of the evil in the world—such was the force of his argument. With logical precision he began a recitation of human history, demonstrating the horrors of inquisitions and holy wars, genocides and civil bloodshed. In our own day there was Northern Ireland, Lebanon, Iran, Sri Lanka, and Pakistan—perhaps even the former Yugoslavia. Make no mistake, the often ugly battles between pro-life and pro-choice factions with regard to abortion amount to violence in the name of religion. Both sides base their righteous judgments upon convictions about what is ultimately true and meaningful. It is often in the name of religion that injury and corruption enter the human story.

What made the evening very uncomfortable was that I was under attack. I almost felt as if I had been set up by my host. For reasons of his own the good philosopher saw me as an enemy—a religious enemy. As is true of many intellectuals, he had no understanding of what a religious studies professor does. He did not realize that those who are most liberated from the errors of religion are those who take it seriously, not those who attack it or rule it out of court. He seemed to have no intimation that I might agree with much of what he said.

Now, I recognize that my adversary may have been playing the philosopher. He may have taken on the wings of the gadfly, the mantle of the agent provocateur, hoping to goad me into an argument. If that was his aim, he was both pompous and presumptuous to assume that he had some ordained privilege to treat me as less than a free human agent. I had not volunteered to be apprenticed to his philosophical discipline. I deserved to be treated as a person in whose eyes one may possibly see the truth of his own selfhood. I prefer to think that he had chosen me as his religious enemy and was out to do battle, to vanquish me in his own holy war.

Recently I picked up the newspaper, only to read one of those sensational items telling about an eighty-five-year-old woman in Buena Vista, California, who was stabbed several times by her live-in nurse during an argument over religion. Husbands and wives still fight about religion. Parents are in conflict with children over religious issues. This warfare continues as it has almost since the dawn of the human race. The Hopi Indians, lovers of peace, fight with their neighbors, the Navajo: they fight about land and its holiness. Greed and the commercialism of the white man's world make war with the Navajo over the San Francisco Peaks—sacred territory for the Navajo, but only valuable real estate to the rest of America. And in the south of Arizona, the Apache nation contends with the Vatican and the University of Arizona concerning the sacredness of Mount Graham and the right to build a giant telescope.

In India, the home of Mohandas K. Gandhi, where thousands of mahatmas have taught peace and lived, trying desperately not to harm other creatures, the Hindus fight with the Sikhs and the Muslims. In Lebanon, Maronite Christians struggle with Muslim factions, who in turn do battle with each other—Sunni and Shi'ite followers of Muhammad engaged in religious strife. There is conflict between sides because of religious identity.

Of course, the struggles are not always bloody, sometimes merely petty and spiteful. For example, there are those who may be members of a Christian church. One of the ways Christian theology describes the meaning of the church is to call it the community of reconciliation. Apparently that was an idea in the minds of the earliest Christians, especially in the thought of Paul.

Let us imagine that a group of eighty people belong to this church in a small village of 500 residents. Suddenly an argument arises over whether an old prayer book should be used, or whether it is more appropriate to use a new one that reflects new ways of addressing new issues that require the attention of common prayer. In addition, there are some members of the community of reconciliation who wish to admit women into their priesthood. Others oppose such a possibility. The result of argument here is schism. There are now two communities of reconciliation in the little village. Yet reconciliation is a principle that reminds these people they belong together. I do not cite this example in order to suggest one faction is wrong and the other right. I cite it to illustrate that the apparently bad things that are done in the name of religion take many forms. Presumably it is unfortunate that two different organizations of one community of reconciliation result from differences of opinion among members.

A very intelligent woman, quite knowledgeable in the arts, once told me that she stopped participating in a church because she had worked hard on many church projects through the years without any recognition of her efforts. No one complimented her. No one expressed any deep appreciation for all she had done. To this woman, a church acts irresponsibly when it ignores people's efforts. To her, "organized religion" is a source of "backbiting," discomfort, and wrongdoing. However, she is the one who acts out of violent motivation.

Juan Padilla, a Spanish Franciscan missionary, lived on the plains of Kansas during the sixteenth century. He had decided to be a teacher and evangelist among the natives. Most missions to the Indians had been accompanied by military escort and weapons, but Fray Juan had developed a love and concern for the natives. He wanted no weapons. He heard that some devout indians still gathered at a cross that had been placed somewhere on the plains by Coronado. There indians still swept clean the sacred space at the foot of the cross and made the signs of prayer that Padilla had taught them.

The friar could not resist such news. He set out to teach them more, taking along flour and wine to celebrate the mass with the natives. But there was more than one tribe on the Plains. There were the Wichita and the Kaw, the Kansas river people—two tribes, two ways of living, two religions. And including the contribution of Juan Padilla, there were three religions. The Wichita liked Fray Juan because he seemed to be a man of great power, magic, and medicine. They confronted the unarmed missionary and tried to stop him from sharing his magic with their enemies the Kaw. The Franciscan ordered his companions to retreat. From a distance one of them saw the indians shoot the venerable Padilla, strip his body, and throw rocks at him until he died.

However, as one historian puts it, the viceroy of New Spain "charged that at a certain hill Spaniards placed Indians in a row to blow them to pieces with cannon fire, to be torn apart by dogs, or to be handed to Negroes who then killed them by knife blows or rope." Dominican missionary and historian Bartolomé de las Casas accused his fellow Spaniards of all kinds of atrocities against the native peoples whose way of living was very different from the conquering Christians.

Why do people do bad things in the name of religion? This is one of the most important questions we can ask. Would it not be better if we avoided religion entirely?

Something about religion disturbs us to the point that most of us consider doing without it. We might say that religion reminds us of something about ourselves that is very disturbing. In the early nineteenth century Henry David Thoreau made this discovery:

> I trust [Thoreau wrote] that some may be as near and dear to Buddha, or Christ, or Swedenborg, who are without the pale of their churches. It is not necessary to be a Christian to appreciate the beauty and significance of the life of Christ. I know that some will have hard thoughts of me, when they hear their Christ named beside my Buddha, yet I am sure that I am willing they should love their Christ more than my Buddha, for the love is the main thing, and I like him too. . . . Why need Christians be still intolerant and superstitious?

There are many ways of asking the question, but it seems as important a query in the latter days of the twentieth century as it was in the early days of the nineteenth. We live in a day of religious resurgence, not decline.

Not long ago I was present at an academic meeting that was addressed by a scholar who devotes his study and thought to interpreting the religious history of black Americans. In attendance at this session were historians and philosophers of religion. In other words these were people who have dedicated their lives to comprehending the nature of religion. I prefer to assume they are also deeply involved in understanding human nature through the study of religion. The visiting professor provided a very effective description of Afro-American history during the period of Reconstruction. He demonstrated how the thinking of black

Christians was influenced by the refusal of white Christians to accept them as unconditional equals—as full participants in the Christian religion and in the American enterprise. Bad things had obviously happened in the name of religion. Black Americans had had to peruse Christian scriptures to find a way of understanding their own suffering as an indication of their special chosen standing in the plans of a provident deity. White Christians had used the same scriptures in order to justify their claims to be separate from and superior to blacks. To the whites a crafty and purposive creator had designed these differences and meant for each people to retain its present status in world history story.

One of the members of the colloquy, a well-known philosopher of religion, began to shake his head in dismay. He raised his hand almost timidly. There was obviously a great sense of helplessness and remorse in his mind. "I wish you could tell me," he pleaded, "why it is that religious people behave that way. But I won't put you on the spot. I'll try to ask another question."

Apparently the good professor was assuming that some people do bad things in the name of religion, while others do not. At that moment he may not have been aware that he was attributing these attitudes and behaviors to *other* people, that he did not see his own self in the eyes of others. I remember that I resolved then and there to write a book that would try to help us deal with this very puzzling aspect of human experience. I found it difficult to believe that a forty-five-year-old scholar of religion had no insight into the dilemma that I have described in this introduction.

This book is not written for scholars of religion. It is written for those people who have wondered about my question. It is especially directed toward those who think they have found an answer without any serious investigation of the history of religions. It is addressed to those who do not participate in religious traditions as well as to those who do. I do not assume my thoughts will satisfy everyone who reads them, but I offer these thoughts because I have spent many years formulating them and have come to take a certain consolation in them. I am deeply indebted to many historians and theologians who have influenced my thinking. They are too numerous to mention and I would not want to neglect any: to neglect a name is to disfigure the mural of memory.

I will mention only one person whose work has had a profound effect upon my thinking. He is not a scholar of religion, but an anthropologist. He has not directly addressed any of his essays to the subject of this book, but he communicates an understanding of human nature that is deeply appreciative of its religious character. I do not hold him responsible for anything I write. Actually, were he alive, he might disagree with many of my ideas. Nevertheless, I offer this book to his memory and conclude this introduction with the words of Loren Eiseley.

> Has the earth's glacial winter, for all our mastery of science, surely subsided? No, the geologist would answer. We merely stand in a transitory spot of sunshine that takes on the illusion of permanence only because the human generations are short.
>
> Has the wintery bleakness in the troubled heart of humanity at least equally retreated?—that aspect of man referred to when the Eskimo, adorned with amulets to ward off evil, reiterated: "Most of all we fear the secret doings of the heedless ones among ourselves."

I Perceive
That You, Too,
Are Religious

If we wish to understand why people do bad things in the name of religion, we must first gain some insight into the nature of religion. As a university professor I frequently ask my students how it is possible that so many diverse ideas and practices in human history can be collected in one basket that is labeled religion. A man sits in the room of a monastery in Tibet. For many years he has been on a quest for Truth. He has studied ancient texts and sat at the feet of great teachers of wisdom in India, Sri Lanka, and finally Tibet. He has spent many hours in meditation and contemplation. Gradually he becomes curiously aware of the room in which he sits.

> Before I knew how it all happened, a majestic human figure took shape before my eyes. It was seated upon a throne, with both feet on the ground, the head crowned with a diadem, the hands raised in a gesture, as if explaining the points of an intricate problem: it was a figure of Buddha Maitreya, the Coming One, who already now is on his way to Buddhahood, and who, like the sun before it rises over the horizon, sends his rays of love into this world of darkness, through which he has been wandering in innumerable forms, through innumerable births and deaths.
>
> I felt a wave of joy passing through me, as I had felt the presence of my spiritual teacher, who had initiated me into the mystic circle of Maitreya and had caused his images to be erected all over Tibet.
>
> I closed my eyes and opened them again; the figure in the wall had not changed. There it stood like a graven image, and yet full of life!
>
> I looked around me to assure myself that I was not dreaming, but everything was as before.

The account goes on to tell in much greater detail the story of this vision. It is an awesome tale by a very respectable and stable scholar. It is not the babbling of a madman, and it leads finally to an outpouring of words akin to poetry. This account belongs to the whole story of religion. It reveals a highly literate and imaginative mind. The effect of the experience is very personal—what might be termed psychological. The individual who gives the account has evidently undergone a kind of transformation. He has discovered meaning and a sense of order in his world that at one time he was not prepared to understand. He has encountered a reality in contrast to what we ordinarily assume to be real. As a result he will now perceive the so-called ordinary world differently. He is like a poet, who seems to perceive sounds and sights that many of us glimpse only partially through his words. This is only one kind of experience that we may observe in the study of religion.

Suppose now that we were to travel to Africa and visit a people known as Akamba. We would discover that children between four and seven participate in a curious ceremony of initiation. When the date is announced, the children are brought by their parents to the designated place. The foreskin of each boy's penis is cut off by a specialist. Each girl has a small portion of the clitoris removed. Men gather to watch the boys and women to watch the girls. The children are expected to endure these painful operations without crying or screaming.

The ceremony is followed by singing, dancing, and drinking beer. It is a festive occasion, but there are also offerings of food and libation to the dead who are assumed to continue living with the community. During the weeks that the wounds are healing, the children are visited by relatives who bring them gifts of money, ornaments, chickens, sometimes even sheep and cattle. What does all this mean? These people live in a world where meaning is derived from a sense of belonging to each other and to the rest of nature by linkage with the dead and the earth's fertility. When the skin is cut from the genitals, one is cut off from childhood and made ready to enter a new stage of existence. The child is no longer ignorant of what life expects of him or her. The blood from the operation flows into the ground and links the child to the spirits of the earth and to those of the community whose bodies have been buried in the ground. In this ritual the children have taken a step toward full participation in a world of order that maintains no great separation between what is visible and invisible.

The transforming vision of the man in Tibet and the initiation ceremony of the Akamba seem to have little in common. Yet to study religion is to study them both.

A student came to visit a Zen master. "When you hear a wooden chicken crow, you will understand your mind," said the master, "Tell me, what does this mean?"

The student replied, "A bronze girl dances to the music of a flute with no holes."

"Ah," said the master, "That is good. Now suppose someone comes to visit our Zen Center, smoking a cigar, and drops ashes on the Buddha. Suppose you are a Zen master, what will you do?"

"I would hit him," said the student.

"Oh, but this person is very strong. He understands that he is Buddha. He is the Way. He will hit you back.

"I would just sit."

"Ah," said the master, "but you are a master. You know that he is attached to emptiness. If you only sit, you will not help him."

"I'm not a Zen master," replied the student. "So how should I know what to do?"

The master and the student had a good laugh. Then the master said, "Practice hard. I hope you soon attain enlightenment."

That is a strange story. Unusual things are said—things that seem to make no sense. The imagination paints a very fanciful setting of master and student, with a great deal of bowing, grinning, and peculiar conversation. We are told this is representative of something called Zen Buddhism. What has this to do with the vision of Maitreya? Or the circumcision of Akamba boys? How is it possible to call each of these a religion?

To the resident of a village in the heart of Sri Lanka or in India it would be an incredible experience to visit a small town in the American heartland on Sunday morning. He would notice that people rise a little later in the morning than on the other days of the week. They dress in their finest clothing and then drive to a white building on the edge of town. The front of the building would have a raised tower, open near the top where a large bell would be visible. As the family approaches the building, the children will walk to a separate but attached wing, while the parents will enter the main doors beneath the tower. If he went inside with the parents, our visitor would notice row after row of dark brown wooden benches. The ceilings will be higher than those of ordinary houses and the windows will have pictures made with pieces of colored glass. The pictures are mostly of a man with a beard who is dressed in robes similar to the monks of Sri Lanka; he seems to be tending sheep. At the front of the room would be a raised platform, and on it a large book, somewhat different in appearance from most other books one sees in America. In front of the reading desk there is a table on which stands a brass ornament, tall like a post with crossbeams, and with some characters engraved at its crossing. On each side of the table there would be an ornate chair with a tall back. A throne for a prince or a chief, perhaps.

The room would soon fill with people and unusual sounds, music resembling tones squeezed out of the horns of buffalo. The people stand together and sing music that is unlike that heard outside on the streets and in the homes. They sing several times during the visit. A man in a black gown takes his place behind the elevated reading desk. Several times he delivers monologues not directed to the people. Most of the heads are bowed, a few stare straight ahead. The man in the black gown smiles. His voice seems a bit unnatural as he changes the course of his words. Now he addresses the people. They listen attentively, some nodding their heads. Others peer into an unknown vision through the panes of colored glass. The man stops speaking. There is more singing and the people leave. At the door there are mumbled pleasantries and shaking of hands. The entire experience is like nothing else one sees in this small town unless, of course, one were to visit another building similar to this one. This, too, is religion.

The Muslim suspends his activities five times a day and recites the Shahāda,

> There is no god except A'llah [*the* God],
> and Muhammad is *the* apostle (prophet) of God.

He performs ablutions in accordance with the command of the Koran. He stands, bends from the hips, prostrates himself, touching his forehead, toes, hands, and knees to the ground, then sits back on his haunches, does another prostration and stands. He recites special words at each stage of his prescribed actions. He does this in a mosque, which means "place of prostration."

How can such diverse ideas and activities all be called religion? What do they have in common? It seems they have nothing in common, but if you will think carefully, you may observe that they are all in some sense "useless." These matters have little to do (directly, at any rate) with eating, sleeping, working, or having sexual relations. It is possible to function physically without being involved in any visions, rituals, special discourses, or other actions called worship or prayer. As biological organisms, it is possible for us to get along without attention to these interests. They have no physical or biological necessity. They are *useless,* or so it seems.

The point is that human organisms appear to transcend their biological nature. That is to say, humans are *more* than biology. Loren Eiseley, archaeologist and naturalist, wrote about the discovery of the remains of Neanderthal humanity in the little French cave near La Chapeile-aux-Saints. These humans, he said, with brains locked in skulls foreshadowing the apes, had "laid down their dead in grief."

> Massive flint-hardened hands had shaped a sepulcher and placed flat stones to guard the dead man's head. A haunch of meat had been left to aid the dead man's journey. Worked flints, a little treasure of the human dawn, had been poured lovingly into the cave. And down the untold centuries the message had come without words: "We, too, whose faces affright you now, knew human agony and human love."

Something about being human seems to stand outside the biological organism. It seeks to make more of existence than mere physical function. It knows "human agony and human love" and tries to make sense of it all. Humankind ordinarily does not leave its dead to rot in the fields or to be carrion for vultures—unless it is being deliberately cruel or has decided that being carrion is in some sense a sacred or holy affair, as in Tibet, or among certain Native American people.

Because we are more than biology, more than physical function, we are open to the possibilities of understanding ultimate order and meaning for our existence. Humans are creatures who are not satisfied with function: they seek meaning. They want to know that their lives are part of a story that gives everything its place, its time, and sense of worth. The story is ultimate because we recognize it is the most important facet of being human, more important than what ordinarily seems to be important. It is this story, this sense of ultimate order and meaning, that makes biological existence worthwhile. To be religious is to be involved in ideas and actions that transcend biological existence to tell a story of ultimate order and meaning. From this observation it is possible to conclude that most human beings are (or have been) religious.

There are, of course, many ways of being religious. Perhaps some are better than others. Perhaps some are true, some false. Some may lead to thoughts and actions that others consider harmful. These possibilities we cannot judge at the moment. What we must be clear about is that human beings, as we have known them up to this moment, have been religious. To be human is to be religious. Unless we become merely functional or mechanical entities, we will try to find ways of proving that we are more than biological organisms, that we have insights and make decisions on the basis of some sense of ultimate order and meaning. That is our religiousness at work.

In order for us to know why people do bad things in the name of religion it is necessary to understand the nature of human religiousness as it has been described above. Once this task is completed, we are ready to take another step. We may now ask: What do people do with their religiousness? In this chapter we shall confine ourselves to an understanding of how religiousness is expressed *outside* the traditional religions to which many people belong.

The well-known American philosopher John Dewey, who greatly influenced twentieth-century education, was one of those learned individuals who felt religion should be avoided *because* people do terrible things in its name. Professor Dewey once wrote:

> I believe that many persons are so repelled from what exists as a religion by its intellectual and immoral implications, that they are not even aware of attitudes in themselves that if they came to fruition would be genuinely religious.

Dewey was a supporter of the "religious" quality of human experience, but he did not like religions. Trust the religiousness that is fundamental to your human nature, said Dewey, but do not permit that religiousness to be imprisoned in the cells of religion. Religion is like hardening of the arteries, according to Dewey. It represents the coagulation of what is otherwise free flowing and necessary to existence. In religion ideas and behavior are confined and repressed to a point where they control us. They no longer serve us; we begin to serve them. We become the servants of doctrine and a certain rigid morality. At that point we are ready to do harm to those who do not agree with our ideas or do not behave morally as we do. If the religious function, Dewey wrote,

> were rescued through emancipation from dependence upon specific types of beliefs and practices, from those elements that constitute a religion, many individuals would find that experiences having the force of bringing about a better, deeper, and enduring adjustment in life are not so rare and infrequent as they are commonly supposed to be.

Dewey asserts, then, that religiousness is good, but our religions are bad. It becomes rather obvious that there is a way of being religious that has little, if anything, to do with religion. Religiousness may be expressed in private experiences and ideas. It may be expressed in activities, games, dances, or special and repeated events like festivals. And it may be expressed in organization, institutions, and associations of people that are not thought to be religions.

Consider a case in which religiousness manifests itself without turning to a particular religion. An imaginary situation: I am interviewing a young man who is employed as a fireman. I discover he has had two years of community college and has decided to spend his lifetime as a fireman. His name is Brad McPherson. I ask him, "Brad, do you belong to any church or religious organization?"

"No, sir!" he replies.

"Is that the result of some decision you have made; or is it just that you haven't thought much about it, or done anything about it?"

"Oh, yeah! I thought about it," he says, "I decided that I'm not going to let anybody tell me what to believe and how to live. I'm a free man!"

"Would you say, Brad, that there is any special meaning to your life? Let me rephrase that question: Is life more to you than just working, eating, and sleeping?"

"Well, now that you mention it—maybe not a whole lot more than that. I'm a fireman, remember? But, no—hey!—I believe that a person has to make the most out of what he's got. I like to take off—you know, like on a day off—if I feel like it, just head for the desert, or the mountains, maybe the Rim Country. Depends on how I feel. I like to get away—someplace where there's no people. Where it's quiet. Sleep under the stars. No tents or cabins—none of that stuff. Just a sleeping bag. Cook some steaks and potatoes over an open fire. Some marshmallows for my wife—she can't get along without them. I just like to be there. Sometimes I hunt a little—whatever's in season. But that's different. It's getting away—being out there. I just—well, it kind of puts everything together. I can go back and do what I have to do. You know, I believe that's what makes this country great. I mean you gotta help people out. Mind your own business. Don't let anybody step on you. And people—they have to learn to do for themselves, too."

Brad does not belong to any religion, any organization, but he is religious. He transcends the biological character of his existence. He has ideas that give ultimate order and meaning to his life. His attitude toward what he calls religion is typically American in being private, independent. Although somewhat ignorant of what religion is—what its most developed ideas and practices mean—he is still religious. He *feeds* his own sense of transcendence by "getting away," gaining a perspective from which he understands not only his own existence, but the entire scheme of things. He mentions no gods/God, no traditional beliefs or practices such as prayer or worship. Yet he is religious by virtue of having a sense of the way things really are and the way things ought to be done. He believes that when he thinks correctly and acts on his understanding of the way things really are, life will have meaning; and he participates in certain rituals that organize his existence and express its meaning.

The psychologist Abraham Maslow believed that a healthy society is made up of individuals who can perceive truth clearly, penetrate falsehood and deception. The healthy society is free of fear and anxiety. It is comprised of spontaneous people who live without artificiality or bitterness. The spontaneous person is able to "let it all hang out." He has no fear of vulnerability. Maslow asks, how can we build a society of individuals like that? One way is to establish therapeutic situations in which people can dig deeply into their own selves. The healthy person knows how to gain self-knowledge and is open to certain special experiences that change the way of looking at existence. These special experiences may sometimes be very exciting, even extraordinary. Some would call them ecstatic peak experiences.

Notice that Professor Maslow avoids references to the languages or formal ideas of traditional religions. You may also observe that he has a vision that transcends the mere functioning of the biological organism. The world is not structured the same way as Maslow's ideal healthy society, but he implies that most of us do not perceive the world as it really is. We need to be made healthy, whole. Maslow's ideas provide existence with ultimate order and meaning.

The artist, musician, even the scientist may provide us with examples of the way religiousness expresses itself. Let us imagine an artist who has nothing to do with churches, synagogues, temples, mantras, or prayer wheels. He reads. He thinks about life. He often finds himself lost in thought, yet he is not really thinking. If someone asked him, "What were you thinking about?" he would be surprised. He would have no response. But he has stored certain impressions, and months later he paints. The picture is of a vast desert, a wasteland without any sign of life. Our eyes come to rest on two shabby posts made out of decaying slats. A piece of flimsy cord is tied between the posts with an occasional thread dangling from its span. The effect is awesome. We feel a curious gnawing in the pit of our stomachs. The artist has titled the painting, "Harnessing Nature." We begin to realize that the artist has stood aside from the routine notions of life, from the ordinariness of existence; and he is expressing what he observed. He illustrates the futility of human assumptions about knowing all there is to know of nature and mastering it. There are no humans visible in the painting, but we may assume that people have erected a very small and fragile fence that they trust is sufficient to harness the vast, foreboding landscape. The artist is searching for meaning that he may affirm. In this painting he seems to be saying that humans delude themselves: they think they have built a meaningful structure, but the results are frail and insignificant. Those people who have some knowledge of the world's religions understand that many of them are based on the idea that much of what we observe and think is real is actually mere illusion.

What we should understand is that the artist is expressing his religiousness. He is doing this as an artist, not as a participant in a traditional religion. Painting is his way of contemplating existence. Both the contemplation and the practice of his art are expressions of his religiousness. Every human who is aware that he is more than a mechanical or functional organism is likely to be concerned with whether life has order and meaning. To make observations and conclusions about that order and meaning is to express our religiousness. It should be obvious that if we wish to understand the effect and influence of religiousness on human behavior, we must look farther than the formal religions. We may or may not agree with John Dewey that *religions* are a source of grief and captivity, but we can certainly agree with him that *religiousness* is a universal human characteristic.

It is important to understand that this religiousness is not only a matter of thinking, belief, or reflection. It is also expressed in actions. The scholar of religion calls some of these actions "rituals." To be human is to be a ritualist. What do we mean by this?

Another story: The man's name is Joel Doughtery. In his own mind he is not a religious person. Of course, that is partly because he does not yet know what we know: that it is difficult to be human and not be religious. Joel works an eight-hour day as a mechanic at Automotive Technical Enterprises. Saturdays he putters around his own car and mows the lawn if his wife exerts enough pressure. Sundays he likes to sleep in, watch a little football, and maybe go four-wheeling with some of the guys. Monday night is special. He comes home from work, kicks off his shoes, and takes a shower. Supper is ready early. Then he goes to the refrigerator to make sure that a few cans of beer are cold and ready. There are sandwich makings in the bin, ham and cheese. Why not make one up in advance? That way it won't take so long to get to it later. On the table next to the Lazy-Boy he sets a dish of taco chips and a basket of pretzels, then cracks open a container of onion dip—all of it for later. He doesn't need it now. He just ate supper. Well, maybe a chip or two.

Joel settles down in the chair, props up his feet, and lets the bulge of his belly push his white T-shirt through the open top of his fly. He is ready for "the game." It is Monday night! He will spend the next several hours in that chair. Watching. Watching and celebrating what is, for Joel, the most important thing in his life. It makes life worth living—football! He eats and drinks, his whole body giving thanks for his favorite teams, his heroes. Their bodies and blood are part of him as he eats and drinks, watches, cheers, and curses. Whether he is at work or out with the guys, football is on his mind; it represents all that it means for him to be alive. It is everything he values. To be a good American. Football is hard work. Competition. Pushing the other guy out of the way. Scoring. Winning. Big bucks. Joel doesn't have big bucks, but he feels that it is all his when he watches Joe Montana, Walter Payton, or Eric Dickerson.

Note: Joel is not a thinker, but he *does things*. He is involved in actions that make no sense if he is only surviving as a functioning, biological organism. That is to say, football is not a matter of basic survival. It is sport. It is something tacked on to mere function by a creature who transcends biological nature. Joel does not *need* the beers, the sandwiches, the chips, and pretzels in order to survive. He may have work that should be done, but Monday night is a special time. Joel is *ritualizing* his existence. By performing certain acts in the same way at a special time, he is celebrating what, for him, gives ultimate order and meaning to life. He may not be doing it consciously, and he would laugh or look bewildered if you suggested he was being religious. However, to those who understand the religiousness of existence, the pattern is clear.

What we have seen thus far is that human beings who do not participate in what we call formal or traditional religions may still express their sense of belonging. Humans find meaning by being able to identify themselves with others. My tribe and clan, my nation may provide me with a sense that life has order, meaning. To belong to someone or something is to know *who* one is, and *why* one is, in the great scheme of things. For some people it would be unbearable to learn that America is not supreme of all nations. America is a sacred order to them. It can do no wrong. It gives all the meaning to life that life can possibly have. And if they acknowledge a god who creates and provides for life, they assume that he/she is the guardian of their own tribe—America.

It is conceivable that I can express my religiousness in my sense of belonging to the Academy of Science, the American Sociological Society, my service club, lodge, or the charity or service agency to which I commit much time and thought. Among many people, such as certain Native American tribes, the order and meaning of life is expressed by belonging to a special animal. The bear, the beaver, the turtle have all served this purpose. My brother or sister, my grandfather or grandmother may be a bear because "my people" have always known that the bear came before us, that his skeleton is like ours—he stands tall and powerful—that he has given his flesh for our survival. It is from his people that our people have emerged. We are the bear people.

Recently a faculty member of my own university, a geology professor, announced he was writing a book attacking creationism. Creationism is an attempt on the part of some Christians to provide scientific support for a literal reading of the Genesis creation accounts. Many intelligent persons may be sympathetic to the professor's enterprise. However, I soon discovered that the professor understands very little about religion or human religiousness. He becomes very religious about something he calls "science." "Science," he is quoted as saying,

> offers truth without certainty. Religion offers certainty without truth. . . . people like to live in a fantasy. They want final truths, but science is tentative. They like to have things black and white, but science isn't black and white—there's a lot of gray.

Notice how the geology professor begins to generalize. The order and meaning of his world are being threatened, and he demonstrates the strength of his own commitments by beginning to say some bad things on behalf of his religiousness. You see, there is no such thing as "science" and there is no such thing as "religion," in the sense the professor uses the terms. There are human beings who are involved in science and religion, who find themselves transcending the world in which they exist, trying to assert whatever ultimate order and meaning they can find. Some scientists offer certainty without truth as they go about their work and thinking. They assume they are dealing with facticity, with what is firm and verifiable. They live in a closed world in which they can acknowledge no other method of finding truth than their own. Something they call "religion" is a threat to the order and meaning of existence as they envision it. They generalize about this evil thing they call religion and in doing so they harm human beings who may express their religiousness in traditional ways. On the other hand, it is obvious that some people who are involved in traditional religion also offer certainty without truth. They may assume that the ultimate order and meaning of their world is divinely established and therefore incapable of false or inadequate interpretation. They are more concerned with the certainty of their enterprise than with learning the possibility that the truth they proclaim is always *more than* our present apprehension or comprehension.

The geology professor may be no more free of doing harm in the name of religiousness than is the creationist. He is not free if he does not understand his own religious nature. He is a victim of the modern attempt to suppress religiousness by confining it to what John Dewey called religion. The professor assumes that religiousness is best avoided or denigrated. He does not recognize in it the high quality of transcendence that is at the heart of the scientific enterprise itself.

We should begin to see that our religiousness is a matter of life and death. To be human is to be religious because we transcend the very nature we attempt to study and control. We are at once free of biological nature, yet part of it. This freedom forces upon us the task of finding some semblance of ultimate order and meaning, and to find such order and meaning is to have a sense of truth and faith in existence.

My religiousness should help me to see a world that is open, expanding, always more than it seems to be. Yet *what it seems to be* is important. It is important that everything that is, everything that *has being,* should have a place in my sense of what the world is all about. My world must have a place for you. It must have a place for those who act as if they were part of another world entirely. If I begin to fence off my world so it has no gates through which I may go out to welcome you, or through which you may enter to greet me, to question me, then I am foreclosing on my religiousness. I am expressing my religiousness in an improper fashion.

However, it is important to understand that I cannot avoid the problem by pretending I am not religious. I can only reject my religiousness if I am willing to give up freedom, my transcendence. To be human is to be constantly faced with the temptation to do bad things in the exercise of our religiousness. I face that temptation as a scientist, a philosopher, a poet, a Buddhist, a Christian, or a Jew. I face it because finding some semblance of ultimate order and meaning is not an easy task. And when I think I have found it, I do not like that order and meaning disturbed by the presence of someone who does not seem to belong. I must understand that the fence posts will always need moving and the gates must always stand ready to be opened. "Something there is," wrote Robert Frost,

> that doesn't love a wall,
> That sends the frozen-ground-swell under it,
> And spills the upper boulders in the sun;
> And makes gaps even two can pass abreast.
> . . . .
> Before I built a wall I'd ask to know
> What I was walling in or walling out,
> And to whom I was like to give offence.
> Something there is that doesn't love a wall,
> That wants it down.

Our religiousness discovers a world that has a horizon, but horizons are always moving. It is fruitless to build a wall on the horizon and expect it to stay there, impregnable, forever.

Religiousness is a high human characteristic; it is fundamental to human nature. It is expressed in many ways that people are not accustomed to call "religion." This religiousness of ours is universal. The bad things that are done in this world are not done because some people are religious and others are not. The violence is not the *result* of the religiousness of people. It stems from those who misunderstand the nature of our religiousness. Remember the geologist's comment: "Science offers truth without certainty. Religion offers certainty without truth"? What he should have said is, There are those people who, in their religious transcendence of their biological nature, are willing to live with moving horizons, knowing the truth without certainty. But there are also those who cannot live with uncertainty, and this often leads them to defensive and hostile attitudes, even violence. They may use science *or* religion to support their violent need for certainty.

How Religiousness Becomes Religion

It may be true, as Robert Frost told us: "Something there is that doesn't love a wall." But isn't it also true that we have been building walls for a long time? Why do we build fences? "Good fences make good neighbors," says the man next door at mending time.

> *Why* do they make good neighbors? Isn't it
> Where there are cows? But here there are no cows.
> Before I built a wall I'd ask to know
> What I was walling in or walling out,
> And to whom I was like to give offence.

We build these fences because we feel the need to wall things in and wall things out. It's often a matter of protection, motivated sometimes by a selfish desire to keep others from having the benefit of the things you call your own.

There is a story about the mullah Nasrudin, a legendary teacher of wisdom. One day a young man followed him to a river bank where he sat down under a tree. The youth watched as the mullah stretched out his hand and a cake appeared in it. Three times he did this. Three times he ate a cake. Then he put out his hand and picked up a goblet and drank his fill.

The young man was so excited that he ran up to Nasrudin, grabbed him by his tunic, and cried out, "Please! Show me how these marvelous things are done. I will do anything you ask."

"Well, my son," answered the mullah, "you must first have the right mind for such things. When that happens, time and space are overcome, and your hand can receive sweets from anywhere. But to find this right state of mind you must follow my way."

"I will do it!" shouted the youth. "Please tell me how."

"There are steps," replied Nasrudin. "You must take them one at a time. Would you like to attempt the easy way or the most difficult one?"

The enthusiastic young man, trying to impress the teacher, replied, "The difficult one! I will take the difficult way!"

"Ah!" said the mullah Nasrudin, "you have made the wrong choice. You should have selected the easy way. But once you have chosen, you cannot change. The difficult exercise is this: make a large enough hole in your wall so that your chickens can get into your neighbor's yard to peck. But the hole must also be small enough to keep your neighbor's chickens from feeding themselves in your own garden."

The business of building walls is a kind of madhouse affair. You are damned if you do and damned if you don't. But mad as it is, it seems to be necessary. After all, I build walls to shut out the driving rain and the blinding snow. The roaches may grind their way through it and the mice hide behind the plaster, but the beasts and thieves of the night are kept out, and the neighbor's dog will not eat my oatmeal.

In the Hebrew Bible there is the familiar story of Jacob, who traveled from Beersheba to Haran. "He lighted upon a certain place, and tarried there all night." The sun had set and it was time to rest. So Jacob gathered some stones and set them up for something to lean against and to protect him from the night. He had a dream. The night got through with its message. He dreamed about a ladder reaching to heaven with angels going up and coming down, and he heard in his dream the voice that sets all things in their proper place. From above the ladder the voice set the directions of north and south, east and west. The dream wrestled Jacob out of his sleep. "This is a holy place," he said to himself. "All things come together in this place. This is a place from which I may see the shape of the world. This is a place of oneness, a place of the Holy One."

Jacob took the stones of his resting place and made a pillar, like the ladder of his dream. He was retracing the journey of his grandfather Abraham. It was a kind of homeward pilgrimage. A person who is on a quest for his roots is searching for his identity in time. Time had come together with this place and he was at the very center of the world. Jacob could look up and down, east, west, north, and south, and feel that he was in the center—the world was all around him. There were four corners, four points in a circle—like a holy temple—and he was ready to organize his existence according to his new presence of holiness, of oneness, order, and meaning. "And this stone, which I have set for a pillar, shall be God's house."

The poet, William Blake, wrote

And every part of the City is fourfold
 and every inhabitant, fourfold.
And every pot and vessel and garment
 and utensil of the houses,
And every house, fourfold.

The walls are built to imitate a discovery of Jacob. Every house we build is a set of walls that are a house of God, a place where time and space come together for us. Inside the walls is a little temple wherein your life is centered, where it finds holiness—wholeness. Some scholars tell us that the oldest houses were the dance houses where the movement of life from place to place in time was fixed by the rhythm of dancers inside the walls; then came the temples, which were houses like Jacob's house. The first churches were dwelling places. Japanese Shinto temples developed out of the simplest houses, Roman temples from the round straw huts of the peasants.

When human beings discover what Jacob discovered, they begin to build walls. Their understanding of who they are and how they fit into the scheme of things is a religious affair, whether it is recognized as that or not. It is part of the quest for order and meaning. When the walls begin to take shape, our religiousness translates itself into religion. We begin to see that the thing we do, the behavior of our lives, and the sense of who we are and to whom we are related take place within walls. Religiousness acted out within walls is religion—whether we call it religion or not.

Like all campuses of twentieth-century universities, the university where I teach has many buildings. They tend to be named for schools and departments, colleges and disciplines that make up this particular universe of education. Of course, the buildings are sometimes named for philanthropists, university presidents, or an occasional professor, but even then the names are attached to a certain enterprise—the Alfred Hamilton School of Fine Arts, the Jordan Education Building. So there are engineering buildings, business buildings, language and literature buildings, and life-science buildings. The College of Law at my university is shaped like a Navajo hogan, though the native dwelling and the law college are "worlds" apart. To enter any one of these buildings is to enter a "world." The building "walls in" a way of believing and thinking, a way of behaving, and a sense that one belongs to a special people. Obviously, this enables persons who inhabit this world to accomplish certain goals. It also tends to serve as the way of providing ultimate order and meaning to existence. Sometimes it is difficult for those in one world to speak with those in another. Arguments are inevitable when a committee tries to make decisions about budgets, curricula, requirements, and the purposes of higher education. The campus becomes a setting for conflicting orthodoxies, each trying to outdo the other. The representatives of many colleges and departments are a kind of priesthood upholding the values of a special constituency. Some of them have sufficient power to inflict undercover violence on those of other persuasions. Here, without special religious labels, we may see violence done in the name of religion.

Elevators provide the setting for strange meetings, even stranger conversations. I have recently been trying to discipline my elevator behavior. It is a difficult assignment. Several people are suddenly thrown together inside a world that measures six feet by six. Most often they know nothing of each other. I make a firm resolve not to watch the lights that signal the ascent into the heavens inside an automated capsule that is not unlike Jacob's pillar. I decide not to look at my own feet; I will look at everyone as a person, eye to eye; and I will say something, if I feel so inclined. But it isn't easy! My resolve frequently dissolves. It is especially difficult if only two people are closed in the shuttle. There is a professor of English that I dread meeting there. He invariably tosses me a comment about religion that disarms me. His gestures are friendly, but the effect is usually awkward. "Hi, Dick!" he greets me, disregarding the fact that I prefer to be called Richard. "How's everything up in heaven? I'm gonna send some students up your way who haven't got a prayer with us. You pray for them."

I can never think of an appropriate reply. I want to tell him that the more religious departments and disciplines of the university tend to be those other than religious studies departments. The academic study of religion disengages our religious temperaments. However, what this professor must understand is that his apparent dissatisfaction with what he calls "organized" religion does not mean that he does not live not in a walled-in world, or that his beliefs and behavior do not form a system that operates very much like a religion.

The Chinese call it the Ten Thousand Li Long Wall. Americans call it the Great Wall of China. It is a monument of human achievement, a wonder of the world that every tourist wants to see. But it is also a shrine of suffering and injustice. It is little wonder that the man who directed its building has been despised by many people. Ch'in Shih Huang-ti was an emperor who lived in the third century B.C.E. The common people have told this story for generations. It seemed the emperor was afraid of the nomads who lived on the Mongolian steppes. He feared these "huns" would overrun the country and steal his wealth and power. He consulted his advisors and decided to build a stone wall along the northern boundaries of his country. But as all builders know, this is not an easy task, not even today. The cutting and setting of stones to make great walls is as difficult for a Chinese emperor as for an Egyptian pharaoh or a king of Israel. The wall of Emperor Shih Huang-ti made little progress. "Ei!" said the counsellor, "the spirits of the wilderness do not take kindly to this. If we want to build a wall that is ten thousand miles long, we must entomb a human being in every mile of it so that his spirit may guard the wall against the spirits of the wilderness."

Well, the emperor took the advice. China was even then a land of many people, and it was easy to arrange sacrifices. Were not the people as plentiful as grass, and was not Shih Huang-ti their master? The plans were made. However, there was a scholar whose conscience bothered him. It would be sufficient, he told the emperor, if one man named Wan were sacrificed. "Wan" means "ten thousand." Wan was enough. The soldiers arrived at the house of Wan, who sat with his bride at the wedding banquet. They carried him away and left his wife, Lady Meng, in great sorrow.

In tears, Lady Meng traveled a great distance to find the place where her husband was buried. At last, on the other side of many mountains and rivers, she came to the wall. How would she ever find her husband's bones? She sat down and wept. It is said the Lady Meng's tears so affected the wall that it broke open and revealed her husband's bones.

Lady Meng Chiang was a famous women. The emperor wanted to meet her, and was so impressed with her beauty and her presence that he wanted her for his wife. Who was Lady Meng to refuse the wishes of the emperor? She could not say no, but she could make certain requests. First there was to be a festival of forty-nine days in honor or Wan; second, the bones of her husband were to be given proper burial and the emperor and his retinue were to be present; and third, there was to be built a terrace forty-nine feet high on which she would make a sacrifice to her husband. The emperor agreed to meet the conditions of Lady Meng.

A hush came over the crowd as Meng Chiang climbed the terrace. Shih Huang-ti listened as she began to damn the emperor for his cruelty and injustice. He held his peace until Lady Meng leaped from the terrace into the river. Then his anger seethed and he ordered his troops to cut her body into pieces and grind the bones to powder. It is said that the soldiers saw only little silver fish where the pieces of her body had been. The soul of the faithful Lady Meng lives in these little silver fish.

This has been a long story about a wall. Few of us would want to say that Shih Huang-ti was wrong to defend himself and his people against invaders. He was perhaps not wrong to think that a wall would help everyone to know the boundaries of the empire. But he was wrong to believe the wall was more important than the people. For without people, what good is it to pretend to be an emperor—an ayatollah, a premier, a pope, a Christ, or a Buddha? A wall is only good so long as people are more important, and sometimes it is only the tears of a Lady Meng—the compassion of a faithful person—that can break down walls of violence.

Humans are builders of walls. As in everything else we do, we may use walls to good effect or ill. My religiousness—that is, my need to discover ultimate order and meaning in existence—expresses itself in three ways, as we have seen in an earlier chapter. Each of these three ways is the foundation of a wall—collecting stones and conceiving a plan. We express our religiousness in ideas, in beliefs or values. We express these ideas in stories or in concepts. Creating stories or teaching reflects an understanding of the need for boundaries and horizons. It is part of distinguishing the self in relation to other creatures and beings. This is our religiousness at work. Yet by itself it is not religion. No walls have yet been erected. There are no sweat lodges, temples, or prayer and study houses. Perhaps it is philosophy or storytelling, but it is not yet religion.

Our religiousness may also lead us to dance, to build sacred things such as masks, prayer sticks, or altars. It may cause us to set aside special times that help us to know the meaning of routine in our existence. The Jewish Sabbath is not like other days; it is not a time to focus on negative things. "The art of keeping the seventh day," wrote Abraham Joshua Heschel, "is the art of painting on the canvas of time the mysterious grandeur of the climax of creation."

The soul cannot celebrate alone, said Heschel, so the body is invited to rejoice in life along with the soul. "Man in his entirety, all his faculties, must share its blessing." The Sabbath says: most of the time you work, but neither work nor efficiency is the purpose of life. You are not a beast of burden. Take this time, which is as no other time, this time that has no usefulness, and celebrate the joy and the vitality of creation.

Whenever we find ourselves setting aside time or performing certain actions in repeated fashion, we are ritualizing, acting out a drama of order and meaning. Here is also our religiousness at work. Therefore, in addition to ideas and beliefs, our religiousness expresses itself in actions, in practices. Yet by itself this form of religiousness is not religion: it is a foundation. Walls are not yet raised, but their significance is entering our consciousness.

It is also true that we get a sense of order and meaning from the discovery that we are related to other persons and places. The lost soul is the one who does not know who he is or where he comes from. Much of the meaning of our lives is derived from a sense that we belong to a family, a town, a nation—or perhaps to a tribe, a church, a special society, or a club. Our religiousness expresses itself socially as well as in ritual, special practices, or in stories and teachings. Yet by itself not one of these expressions is religion. When all *three* expressions of our religiousness are present in some coherent fashion, it is possible to recognize a particular way, an identifiable arrangement or scheme. We become aware of walls that help to define and preserve. We may identify these ways as those of the Hopi, the Akamba, and the Jews, or the Buddha. There may even be special buildings whose walls demonstrate the notion of existence represented by one way. Religions are walls erected based on our quest for order and meaning. And building walls is inevitable and good as long as people are more important than walls. When it is the other way around, bad things may be done in the name of religion. We may begin to see the husband of Lady Meng immured in a wall. Then it is time for protest and for tears on behalf of our religiousness.

When a person comes to me and says, "I am a Buddhist," she is telling me that she understands her world in a particular way. She has special ideas, engages in special practices, behaves in a certain way, and identifies with a distinctive community. All three expressions of her religiousness belong together and are derived from a common history. Her religion is Buddhism. However, if she has merely read certain literature that belongs to Buddhist history and has been influenced by Buddhist *ideas*, we might not consider her a member of Buddhism as a religion. Her religiousness may be informed by Buddhist doctrine. Still, if she does not engage in any special practices and does not find meaning in being identified by the beloved community of the Enlightened One (the Buddha), she is not a Buddhist.

Now suppose I drive north from Phoenix on Interstate 17 in Arizona.

As I pass through Flagstaff on Route 89 I begin to enter a world where the desert is more barren than the saguaro lands to the south. There are rocks and canyons. The vegetation is sparse. Long stretches of sunlit granite sands shimmer on the horizon. Occasionally I may see a curious figure resembling a ghost, as if a picture had come to life out of an old Western film or an issue of *Arizona Highways* magazine. In the distance a pony ambles across the wasteland, his rider a native shadow, his broad-brimmed hat and braided hair lingering in my mind as I drive toward Tuba City. Soon I arrive at old Oraibi on the third mesa of the Hopi reservation. The Hopi are pueblo or village people. Their ancestors came into the Southwest more than 2,000 years ago. They have been farmers since ancient times, growing corn, beans, and squash.

If I stay long enough I will hear stories of how they emerged out of the dark womb of Mother Earth. Inside the kiva, the sacred pit house, I could see the great hole in the ground (the sipapu) that reminds the people of their emergence from the primordial underworld regions. And on a rock to the south of the village there is another symbol of the womb of Mother Earth, with its opening intersected by a cross line: this is the umbilical cord that connects the Hopi to their origins.

As I listen to the stories and observe the arrangement of the village, its homes, and daily life, I become aware that certain ideas expressed in stories and symbols form the very heart of Hopi existence. If my visit is made at the right time, I may see a dance of the kachinas. The kachinas are the venerated spirit friends of these people. They are the stars, the plants and animals, the minerals, the living dead. They are present in the masked dancers who visit the village in the winter and spring of every year. I watch the ceremony during the winter solstice. Every person in the village breathes upon a husk of corn and sends a message to the spirit beings who are the powers of fertility. The male corn collector simulates the action of sexual intercourse. Then the seed corn is gathered from the people and blessed. I follow the action to a kiva where the kachina of vegetation leaps and dances around the hole from which Hopi life emerges. Every house in the village receives a prayer stick, the very presence of which is a standing prayer for fertility during the coming months. If I were to observe the actions of these people throughout the course of a year, I would perceive that they were maintaining the harmony of the universe.

The Hopi are a special people, a chosen people. They have come from three previous worlds to the present fourth world, and they have

migrated over this continent until they came to their predestined homeland, whose center is present-day Oraibi, Arizona. The Hopi are a
peaceful people who belong to the earth and to one another. They
comprise many clans—the Badger, the Bear, the Sun, Coyote, Snake,
Reed, Water, and Cloud. The very meaning of their existence and the
order that is fundamental to it are present in their people. To be Hopi is
to know oneself in the scheme of things. The meaning of existence is an
affair of belonging.

Until white men and women came with their pretense to scientific
knowledge and need to classify what they observe, the Hopi would not
have thought of their way of life as a religion. Theirs has not been a
world religion that seeks to convince others of the necessity of becoming
a Hopi, or even one that promises special wisdom. Yet we observe in the
Hopi way of living those three expressions of ideas, actions, and social
identity that together constitute a religion. The walls of the pueblos and
the kivas symbolize a special way of life, an *identifiable* way.

The Hopi reside in a special world, one of the most inhospitable
landscapes in America. Yet they live in harmony with their universe.
Today there are land disputes with the Navajo. The United States government is rearranging and redistributing the lands. The peaceful Hopi are
unhappy. There have been some skirmishes. Why? Is it a simple property
dispute, in which I claim you are trespassing on what belongs to me? We
should understand that it is a religious matter. The place where the Hopis
reside is sacred space. It is the promised land to which they have been
led. It would be very wrong for us to say to these people: "Why fight
over arid wasteland? You will get other homes, other land, in return for
your former property. It's a good exchange." To think such thoughts as
these would be to ignore the walls that are important to their well-being,
their sense of ultimate order and meaning. More than that, it would be to
make war on them because we have in mind a different set of walls.

The San Francisco mountains rise majestically across the skyline just
north of Flagstaff. One can see their snowcapped peaks for many miles
around. They are a very impressive sight for the motorist who rides the
interstate trail northward from Phoenix and the Valley of the Sun. They
are on the edge of the sacred worlds of the Hopi and the Navajo, and
they are very important to those worlds. For the Hopi it is in the peaks
that the kachinas dwell during the second half of the year. It is from
those peaks that they will come back into the Hopi villages, bringing the
powers of fertility and the sacred energies that make life possible.

The beliefs and values of the white person's world are different. Those mountains are a "resource." They can be a place for skiing and recreation. They become something to be used, exploited, controlled. They are commercially attractive and must be developed. The ultimate order and meaning of the white person's world is determined by his belief that he does not belong to the green world of plants, animals, and minerals. He believes he is outside that world, that he is the creator of his own world, his own destiny. It must be emphasized that he *believes* these things and that the beliefs take shape based on his view of the world.

Our entire technological and consumer mind-set is religious; moreover, it even becomes a religion. It would be easy to demonstrate how technology and consumerisn are supported by beliefs, ideas, symbols; how we celebrate the life they represent by certain rituals and ceremonies; how our institutions and social identity are shaped by these ideas and practices. What is more, we are vigorous and militant in our defense of this religion. We evangelize the world in its behalf. The golden arches of McDonald's rise like temple vaults in almost every corner of the earth. We do very bad things in the name of this religion. We violate the sacred space of the natives of the Amazon rain forests, where we destroy the trees to make way for the cheap grazing of cattle that provide the beef for hasty hamburgers. We exploit and desecrate the sacred space of the Hopi. We do violence to the Hopi people, who are transformed into the poor, the alcoholic, the obese in their efforts to live on the boundary between our world and their own. They are immured as was Meng Wan, in the walls of an empire.

Doing bad things in the name of religion is not an easy problem to solve. There are those who would solve it by saying: Have nothing to do with religion; religion is the cause of most of the trouble in the world. For example, they would point out that overpopulation is mostly the result of religion and superstition. It is true that some religious traditions oppose all forms of killing. A Jain tries to avoid tramping on an ant or drowning bacteria in his breathing and swallowing. It is also true that Roman Catholicism defends the creative and procreative process by rejecting artificial means of birth control. But much overpopulation is the result of ignorance and a failure to take responsiblhty for human actions. It is possible to live in the light of traditions like Jainism or Roman Catholicism without contributing to the overpopulation of the earth.

If I am a Roman Catholic, I am responsible for living in the world the Catholic tradition represents. Inside the walls of the Catholic way is the insight that the world has been set in motion by the will of a personal creative energy—a creator. It is the intention of this creator that the world shall be constantly replenlshed by procreation. If procreative acts are accomplished in their season, they lead to birth. Nothing artificial should interrupt this creative process. If I have reverence for the creative process, I will learn to honor its ways. Just as I will not plant seed corn in the spring unless I intend to harvest the corn later on, so I will not fertilize the ovum of a woman at her times of fertility unless I intend to foster the process of human birth. I may not belong to the Catholic way; I may live outside its walls. But it is a perfectly logical and honorable structure.

We live in a time when the walls of our religiousness are crumbling. Horizons and frontiers are changing, and many existing walls no longer represent the real boundaries of our existence. "Something there is that doesn't love a wall," though walls are good and necessary so long as they serve people. Still, the walls that separate religions in our time are difficult to maintain. It is one thing when the wall can be a Great Wall and those outside can be thought of as unenlightened, heathen, barbarian. In such circumstances the Hopi way remains on the mesas of Arizona, just as one Buddhist way remains in Sri Lanka and Thailand, another Buddhist way in Tibet, and still others in Japan. The Christian way remains in Europe and America.

But what happens when Buddhist and Christian and Hopi live next to each other outside old walls? Some people will be frightened when they realize what is happening. They may become defenders of walls, rather than students of the truths that the old walls preserved. There may be violence, but nothing will restore those old walls—something there is that does not like them to be permanent.

In the days of crumbling old walls, human religiousness is in a state of confusion and radical change. We therefore find it expressing itself in ways that are not traditionally religious. Our technological and consumer society functions as a religious establishment. Certain scientific and political movements function as religion. Marxism and other forms of communism are surrogate religions: they are religiousness at work in nontraditional ways, building new walls that house the substitutes for the great religious traditions of our history. And there wiil be violence committed by the devotees of new "religions."

It should be obvious that the religious competition of our day will occasionally lead to violence. It should also be obvious that none of us is exempt, by reason of some supposed nonreligiousness, from involvement in the violence. We must remember that violence is covert as well as overt. Overt violence is the kind of open confhct that occurs when Protestants and Roman Catholics encounter each other in Northern Ireland, or when Jews are exterminated in the pogroms of Eastern Europe or the Nazi death camps. But there is another form of violence that is subtle, unrecognized, covert. When European nations moved into the great continent of Africa and imposed a way of life on the black residents, the assumption behind it was this: we are civilized, and you are not; our beliefs and values, derived from our worldview, are not only superior to yours, they are the way into which you must be initiated. This assumption brought force (overt violence) to bear upon the religious traditions of Africa, but it also produced *covert* violence in schools and industries where the natives' traditional ways were suppressed or ignored. When our choices about how we will live and work are controlled by an emperor or a system, violence will be done.

The religion of technological society produces covert violence when, for example, it gives people little freedom of choice as to whether they will enter the world of computerization. To devotees it is a foregone conclusion that computers are a good thing and that our lives should be regulated by their use. They represent a way of life that is not tolerant of other ways of life. It is not possible for me to say "I'm sorry, but I do not wish to live in a world where computers shape my values and beliefs." If I make such a statement, I must be prepared for oppression or escape to some dark corner of the earth. It is not possible for *some* people to be computerized, others not. Computerization demands the world's obedience. It permits no heresy, though it may be destroying much that is humanly valuable.

Covert violence takes place in many parts of the world because emperors of technology and industry look upon people as grass and weeds. They build great walls out of their new systems of truth and the good life. They believe that whatever is possible must be done, that whoever has the genius to achieve a certain goal is justified in his advantage over others. Seventy-five percent of the world's resources are controlled by eighteen percent of the world's population. Two-thirds of the world's population suffer poverty in the exploitative system of those who believe they are justified in doing what they do, that they are either the world's self-appointed gods or God's special commissioners. The latter days of 1984 were shattered by many incidents of violence. One incident occurred in Bhopal, India, where overt violence was the result of a way of life imposed upon residents of that city. The representatives of an American corporation had been involved in *covert* violence long before the gas explosions. They had assumed they had a right to serve their own ends by taking advantage of the economical needs of the Indians. They erected their walls without regard to the needs.

Another incident of violence, also in india, was the assassination of Prime Minister Indira Gandhi. Her murder was apparently the result of centuries of religious unrest in the subcontinent of India. It was part of a struggle between people who call themselves Sikhs and those who remain loyal to the ancient ways of the Hindus. Many Sikhs, who are primarily residents of the Punjab, have become separatists: they want independence from Hindu India. This is another case in which people of one religion find it difficult to live with those of another religion. Walls are erected and defended.

The solution is simple, you say: people must transcend their narrow religious horizons. They must rise above their petty and fanatical ways. Or you may take a more radical, *seemingly intelligent* position: if people had nothing to do with religion, then there would be no problem. However, we have already seen that those who ignore the traditional religions cannot escape the religious need to live in a world of ultimate order and meaning. But let us return for a moment to the first response. If we look into history we will discover that virtually every new religion was based partly on the conviction that people must rise above their petty fanatical ways.

For example, in the subcontinent of India, during the fifth century, there lived a man named Nānak. In those days tensions existed between people of two religions, Hinduism and Islam. Nānak belonged to a Hindu family but he had friends and associates who were Muslim. He observed many bad things that happened in the name of religion. It is said he was a poet by nature, given to meditation and reflection upon the human story and its meaning. One day he disappeared into the woodlands, where he was transformed by an experience. When he emerged from the forest, he remained silent for one day, and on the next he uttered the pregnant pronouncement, "There is no Hindu, there is no Mussulman [Muslim]." Thus began a campaign that was directed toward the reform and reconciliation of different religions. Nānak believed religion should improve the conditions of existence by compassion, virtue, dedication, and concerted effort. Nānak was an enlightened person. Nānak was the founder of Sikhism.

When the news of Indira Gandhi's assassination reached the United States, our pundits and sages rose to the occasion. They offered their explanations and prescriptions. One commentator said something to this effect: "This struggle is not really a religious struggle; it is geographical." He went on to explain about the Punjab—how it is different from the rest of India and marked by the course of a unique geographical history. That analysis reveals the failure of Western academics and intellectuals (Westerners in general, for that matter) to understand the nature of religion. Religion, we should know, is as much a matter of geography as it is anything else. Religion has to do with one's *place* in the world, and with the manner in which the world is meaningfully put together. Religion is the ordering of space and time. Sometimes it is even a matter of *special* geography, *special* space, as in the case of Israel, or of the Hopi mesas, or even of America itself.

Another very respected editorialist had a comment to make in explaining Gandhi's death. This jounalist is someone we might expect to be more familiar with the religious nature of humanity, with the nature of religion itself. Yet his comment also missed the mark: "It is obvious," he said, "that the world's problems will never subside until we get religion out of politics."

Now, if he meant to bemoan the way rulers of one religious persuasion can force their convictions on the people of another, we may have some sympathy with his point of view. However, there is another sense in which religion and politics are inseparable. Politics has to do with the manner in which human society (the polis, the city) is governed. If I have certain beliefs and values concerning the ultimate order and meaning of existence, they are directly relevant to my government. How could it be otherwise? Therefore, my religiousness has political implications.

If my religiousness can be identified with a particular religion, if I live in a world that is informed, for example, by Sikhism, Hinduism, Christianity, or secular humanism, then my political ideas and practices will be shaped by that sense of the world. "Good fences make good neighbors." If I say that I have no religion, then all you need do is discover the beliefs and values I actually hold and you will understand how my religiousness affects my politics.

This chapter has pointed out that the presence of all three forms of religious expression constitutes a religion. When we are conscious of our religions as a special "way," we may be prepared to defend them or promote them in some fashion. However, our religions may be as unacknowledged as our religiousness. That is to say, we may be representatives of worldviews, of ways of understanding the ultimate order and meaning of existence, without being aware of it. And we may reject any suggestion of religiousness or religion. Nevertheless, call it what we may, the results are the same. We should begin to understand that doing bad things in the name of religion is not a rare and ugly occurrence attributable only to those "stupid and fanatical folks" who bear a religious label. Most of us are involved in the same circumstances. Perhaps all of us do bad things in the name of (or as a representative of) religion. Once we begin to understand this, we shall be in a better position to rise above the more inhumane and immoral manifestation of religion. We will do fewer bad things in the name of religion once we understand what religion is, and become constructively accountable for our own religiousness.

Religions Exist *because* People Do Bad Things

Henry David Thoreau once said that "disease is the rule of existence," that we are all "wreckers [who] . . . contract the habits of wreckers."

The huge oak trees of the Arizona Rim Country are sky scratchers. They raise a thousand fingered nails across the clouds. I walk out into the autumn chill and watch the puffs of vapored breath mock the rising of wood smoke. The stove in my cabin is an Ashley. It can take the chunks of pine, or oak and juniper, and transform them into raging fire. But the Ashley softens the rage, makes them burn long and slowly. The smoldering wisps climb out of the chimney and scale the towering limbs of the sky-scratching oak trees. The trees look healthy enough, but for every green and lusty branch there are many dry and craggy twigs. Whole limbs press somber outlines, like burial markers, across the coming twilight.

The trees are majestic, but they also have riddled leaves; worms ply their ugly trade inside trunks and through the branches. Yet worms have no particular malice. It is a rule that life must feed upon life. Nothing is quite what it seems to be. It is so much more. Every judgement I make about someone else's behavior is bound to be tainted by my failure to acknowledge this. I prefer to live with the illusion of my own accuracy of judgement. Therefore, I seldom remember that the other person is not as bad as I make him out to be, and that I am not as good (or intelligent) as I prefer to believe.

When I was a boy, one of my uncles had an air rifle. It used BBs, but you could pump the thing to unimagined pressure. It was a lethal weapon. I remember one uncle shooting at a target—he was aiming in the direction of the feed-house door. Another relative innocently crossed the line of fire and took a BB in his ankle. It took some carving by old

Doc Haberman to get it out. I inherited the gun. I loved to shoot. Still do. We used to take cans and bottles to the old quarry, float them on the water, and try to sink the cans and smash the bottles. We also went to the dump, where there were plenty of rats and mice. There I learned the thrill of destroying life. Unwanted life. Low life. The air rifle helped to make destruction a harmless game. Sometimes there were birds lined up on the telephone wires. They were only sparrows, or grackels. Who needed them anyway?

I now have another air rifle. It shoots pellets as well as BBs. I haven't used it much. It's for target shooting, for aiming at cans and bottles. I am a "mature" man now, and very much opposed to violence, to the unnecessary destruction of life—any kind. Yesterday I noticed the rifle. It stood in a corner of my study. I picked it up and opened the door. There is an aluminum can that hangs from the bottom limb of an orange tree. I aimed. Then, out of the corner of my eye, I caught a glimpse of the birds. They queued up on the power lines. The rifle rose slowly and beaded their shiny black feathers. They were like vultures. There were too many of them. Someone has to maintain the balance of nature. One less dirty bird would hardly matter. Then I pictured the warm-blooded corpse, lying on the ground, pulsating with its ebbing flow of life. I lowered the rifle. At that moment I couldn't pull the trigger, but I knew I was still a killer.

Loren Eiseley wrote touchingly of Neanderthal humanity. Those creatures, "whose brains were locked in a skull foreshadowing the ape, these men whom scientists had contended to possess no thoughts beyond those of the brute, had laid down their dead in grief." Their hands had shaped a sepulcher and set down stones to guard the head. A chunk of meat was left to nourish the spirit on its journey. And gifts of flint were placed in loving care inside the grave. Fifty thousand years have not altered the importance of that act. "It is the human gesture," writes Eiseley, "by which we know a man, though he looks out upon us under a brow reminiscent of the ape."

Eiseley is right. The Neanderthal also took his axe to the head of his enemy. This is also a human gesture by which we know ourselves, whether we are professor, physician, Mafia hitman, insurance executive, or construction worker. Anyone who does not recognize the presence of both gestures in himself is neither honest nor wise. "We are all wreckers," though we are not *entirely* wreckers. "Disease is the rule of existence," though we also make gestures of love and concern. We are never far from the worms and riddled leaves, even though nature's beauty makes us smile and the fleeting moves of the white-tailed buck take our breath away.

It may be, as Plato says in the *Timaeus*, that the whole process of creation is for the purpose of shaping and adapting the material order to spiritual ends. We may have a dire responsibility for making all of life responsive to Eiseley's "human gesture" of love. Perhaps ours is indeed a spiritualizing task, but we labor against forces, even in ourselves, that seek chaos rather than order.

When I contemplate the situation of my own existence, I realize not only that there are both kinds of human gesture present in me, but also that I am judging myself and the world in which I live. In other words, I know that I am capable of giving assistance to the person who lies wounded by the side of the road or that I can give a basket of food to the family that would otherwise have no Thanksgiving dinner. I also know that I am often guilty of spiteful acts against the person who has deprived me of a raise in my salary. There is something else I know that is perhaps more important. I know I am not what I should be. Ever. I know there is a gap between what ought to be and what is. That gap exists in me, in others, in the world, even in nature. It is a fact of existence, inescapable. Being human makes it possible for me to be aware of this gap. My awareness of it may be an illustration of Plato's point that we are meant to shape the material order to spiritual ends; and I must be conscious of the fact that it is not already shaped to those ends.

Knowing that both kinds of human gesture are present in us, and knowing that there is a gap between what ought to be and what is, human beings have discovered a variety of ways to deal with these facts. We call these ways religions. A religion should be judged by the manner in which it enables us to deal successfully with our existence and its problems. That is, instead of making self-righteous judgements that people continue to do bad things even though they are religious or identified with a religion, we should begin to see that a religion is good and reasonable to the extent that it enriches the lives of people who are always doing bad things. People do not immediately cease doing bad things by virtue of their being religious. Instead they tend to take their religiousness seriously to the extent that they know that the world is not as it should be. A truly religious person is one who recognizes what Paul once said: "I can will what is right but I cannot do it. For I do not do the good I want, but the evil I do not want is what I do." He might well have added: "And often, I find myself doing the good I had not intended. Sometimes I even do what I intend—both good and evil. That is my condition. Is it not also yours?"

There is a story frequently used in the American pulpit. The pastor meets a resident of his town. They stop to pass the time of day. "How is it that we never see you at Sunday services?" asks the pastor.

"Oh, pastor, I know the people who attend your services. They are all people who say one thing and do another. They go to worship on Sunday, confess their sins, then do all kinds of terrible things the rest of the week. There are just too many hypocrites in the church."

The pastor replies, "Ah, but my friend, there is always room for one more."

Some might say the church is the community of hypocrites—those whose intentions outstrip their lives. While the story may seem trivial, it is nevertheless profound. It communicates a truth every sensitive person understands: the gap between what ought to be and what is is never bridged absolutely, at least not in our ordinary human experience. Good and evil gestures are continually present. Our religiousness recognizes this and searches for a way to deal with it. An effective religion will help us to deal with the gap that remains, the evil gestures ever present, even when we don't intend them.

Sometime before the end of the sixth century B.C.E., probably 563, a son was born to a petty chieftain of the Sakya clan at Kapilavastu, about 130 miles north of Benares in the northeastern section of the subcontinent of India. The son was to be called Siddhārtha; Gautama was his family name. Tradition says his father hoped he would become the emperor of all India. He was probably raised in luxury: "I wore garments of silk and my attendants held a white umbrella over me." His youth passed in the ordinary manner of life in a privileged family. He married a neighboring princess. Yet Siddhārtha became more and more dissatisfied with his life. In his late twenties his wife bore him a son and he decided to "go out from the household life and into the homeless state." In the prime of his life, "with a wealth of coal-black hair untouched by grey . . . [he] cut off [his] hair and beard, [and] donned the yellow robe."

Legend tells us Siddhārtha's father had kept him from seeing the plight of the aged and the sick. He had been raised in ignorance of the common fate of humanity in which old age, disease, and death are constant and imminent experiences. One day the gods decided to take a hand in this affair. They sent one of their own to assume the forms of a feeble old man, a diseased man, and a corpse on its way to a funeral pyre. Siddhārtha was startled by these appearances. He had never seen such awful sights. They robbed him of his peace of mind: "I also am subject to decay. . . . Is it right that I should feel horror, repulsion, and disgust when I see another in such plight? And when I reflected thus. . . . all the joy of life . . . died within me." It was this discovery that turned him on his quest for a peaceful soul and freedom from the miseries of existence.

Siddhāartha sought out a variety of teachers and tried many styles of meditation and philosophy. For six years he gave himself to forms of self-denial that tested his physical endurance to its limits, but there was no peace. These practices wasted the body without bringing enlightenment. So in his thirty-fifth year he sat alone one long night at the foot of a fig tree. "Though skin, nerves, and bone shall waste away, and lifeblood itself be dried up, here sit I till I attain Enlightenment." All his determination seemed at an end. What was he to make of his life? Was it possible to find an answer to the riddle of existence?

Then suddenly—release! A flash of insight! It was desire that prevented freedom from suffering! By that illumination he became Buddha, the enlightened One, the Tathāgata. At first he thought he would cherish his enlightenment and keep it to himself; however, it became evident that such an impulse was itself the offspring of desire. Soon his discovery led to compassion for the world and he became a wandering teacher. Converts gathered around him until he founded the Sangha ("community"), an order of disciples who lived for the most part in communities, procuring one meal a day by begging with an alms bowl, practicing meditation and confession, keeping the tradition of the Buddha's lessons, and waiting for the gift of enlightenment.

Siddhārtha's story tells of the formation of a religion. It begins with a religious quest, a search for some sense of ultimate order and meaning. It is completed by the formation of a way, a path, what is called Dharma ("what is established" = "law"); and a group of followers (the Sangha) comes into being. Four Noble Truths are at the heart of Siddhārtha's enlightenment and became the formula for Buddhist teaching: (1) Suffering, (2) the Cause of Suffering, (3) the Necessity of Escape from Suffering, (4) the Way to Escape from Suffering. When Siddhārtha began to observe the common circumstances of existence and realized that he, too, shared those circumstances, he was face to face with suffering. We suffer not merely because our nervous system transmits messages of pain, but also because we wish it were not so. Our minds, our consciousness tell us that such suffering should not be, and so we suffer because we sense the gap between what ought to be and what is. Siddhārtha realized that our suffering is caused by desire. If we could be raised above our expectations, our desires, then we would discover that suffering is the result of a dream, an illusion that the self is important. We would be enlightened and overcome suffering by passing quietly to Nirvana—the state that is no state, the knowledge that is knowledge of nothing, no self.

Siddhārtha's religious quest and his discovery of a formula that offers a solution to the dilemma of existence are both based upon the common human experience that things are not as they should be. I do not act as I should act. Something seems wrong and evil in the realms of nature where death and disease run rampant. If I discover, as Siddhārtha did, a path that helps me pass through this swamp of good and evil, it does not necessarily follow that the world will no longer be the setting of evil and suffering. It does not mean that I will no longer be a *contributor* to the evil and suffering I see in the world. I may not consciously do bad things *in the name* of religion, but if I am not willing to suffer rather than to return evil for evil, I will be contributing to the bad things that are done. If I were to come to the conclusion that you are ignorant and evil because you will not acknowledge the superiority of my special path, my unique insights and practices, then I may very well begin to do bad things in the name of my religion. However, the path itself (the religion) will not be at fault; rather it will be a means of understanding the *reason* for my bad actions. It will help me live with the dilemma. For remember, according to Siddārtha, evil and suffering are the result of desire, which is a way of willing, thinking, and acting under the illusion that the self really exists. A good religion will show us why people do bad things—whether in the name of religion or out of intended or accidental evil. According to Siddhārtha, when people do evil in the name of religion it is because they have not been released from desire and the illusion of the separate self.

Another story, this one more familiar to Americans and Europeans. Almost 2,000 years ago there emerged from among people of his time a young man who was greatly concerned about the welfare of poor people who had little to eat and who lived at the mercy of indifferent Roman rulers and petty local magistrates of his own kind. He wondered why this had to be. At first he questioned whether it might not be best to find some power to match the power of the oppressors. Would it not be best to liberate the oppressed by force? His answer was no: such actions would only contribute more evil and violence. He pondered other possibilities. Like all of us, he considered the possibility of using his talents to achieve his own upward mobility—to become a leader, to beat the system and become wealthy himself. The thought even came to him that he might have supernatural powers, that he might lead people out of their misery by trading on the mysterious energies of God's universe. Self-esteem. Positive thinking. Goal setting. Miracles.

He thought about these problems for some time. He had been born and raised a Jew in a tiny province in the Eastern Mediterranean territory of Palestine. He was a student of the Torah and the Prophets. Some of his people believed that the evil and suffering in the world were the result of not abiding by the special laws and practices that God had demanded of his people long ago. They believed they could rise above the evil and suffering of the world by the study and practice of the special way—the Torah. Torah governed relationships between God and His people and their relationships with each other. Some Jews felt evil and suffering would only cease when God decided to alter the course of time by sending a special leader who would restore the golden age of the second ruler. There were differing points of view concerning what kind of leader would emerge. Some felt he would be a representative man, a man who personified the Torah. Others wanted him to be a military leader who would rid their land of enemies. It is quite natural that people who are oppressed should want to overthrow their oppressors. It is also natural for them to assume that their own path (religion), their own way of life, provides them with a righteous cause that helps them to justify doing harm to others in the name of justice.

The young man in our story knew all about the traditions of his people. He also understood their plight and their feelings of helplessness and anger. However, he had just undergone an unusual experience. He had been attracted to the teachings of a prophet called John the Baptizer. John's message had said that the coming of the special leader, the Messiah, was at hand. There was already evidence—signs of the end of the present age; and the Messiah was already cleaning up the "threshing floor, preparing to store his wheat in the barn." People responded to John's message by being immersed in the Jordan River as a sign of their repentance and preparedness for the new beginning, the new world of the Messiah. John instructed his baptized followers that they were to live in very strict personal and social discipline. "What ought we to do as we wait for the Messiah?" they asked. "The man who has two shirts," said John, "must share with the man who has none, and the man who has food must do the same."

The young man, Jesus, became one of John's followers; at least the story tells us of his baptism under John's hands. For him it was a profound experience. His life took on a curious sense of purpose. Like Amos, Isaiah, and Jeremiah before him, the young man had known, through baptism, the double experience of mystic illumination and the call to perform a special teaching role.

At first Jesus tried to carry on in the tradition of John, who was imprisoned and finally executed for condemning the illegal marriage of the puppet ruler Herod Antipas. "There is good news," he proclaimed. "The special time has come. The rule of God is near. Repent and believe this good news!" He knew in his own mind that the evil and suffering of the world would come to an end when God rules rather than humans. Humans are so concerned for their own individual welfare that they pass by others in need and often deliberately do evil to others for personal gain. God does not intend this kind of world. Thus there is a gap between what ought to be and what is. God bridges that gap by substituting his reign for the reign of the self.

Unusual things began to happen. When Jesus taught in the local synagogue, it seemed as if an authority not of his own desire was asserting itself. He seemed to *embody* the teaching he shared with his audience. Then another astonishing thing occurred. A man in the assembly who believed there was a devil in him that caused his abnormal physical and psychological condition suddenly interrupted Jesus. "What do you want of us, Jesus, you Nazarene? Have you come to destroy us? I know who you are, you are God's Holy One!"

Jesus reproved him, and said, "Silence! Get out of him!"

"The foul spirit convulsed the man and gave a loud cry and went out of him."

The story continues with incident after incident evidencing a special power that brought healing and hope to people who were otherwise hopeless. Jesus' followers, and apparently even some of the general public, began to conclude that he was the Messiah. When he refused to use the methods of force and power associated with a revolutionary leader, some decided that he could not be the Messiah. However, there were those who began to revise their understanding of what kind of role the Messiah should play. They saw in the young teacher the embodiment of a new age, a new way of living and thinking. He was the teacher of a special righteousness, and he used his life as its example. His message was not self-consciously a new doctrine.

The Roman authorities began to see him as a menace. His teaching about the special rule of God made them think he might become a threat to the political order, the Pax Romana. Perhaps he would be proclaimed king of Judea. Of course, the petty rulers of his own people thought Jesus was presumptuous, that he would upset the delicate balance of their own power. Many people wanted him to liberate them from the oppressive taxation and the feeling that their homes were no longer their own. There was a great deal of confusion associated with the young teacher: some loved him and found their lives given hope and health. Some were threatened; others were jealous. Still others were disappointed.

The outcome of the situation was that Jesus was arrested, brought to trial as a common criminal, and finally crucified. He was nailed to a cross, a punishment reserved for slaves and those who could not prove Roman citizenship.

Jesus' followers realized that the same authority, the same power of hope and healing that was the measure of his life, overcame his death. They believed that God had seen to the resurrection of the teacher of truth and righteousness, the true son of humankind. Soon many others began to share this same experience and another great religion was born.

Central to the story of the Christian faith is the knowledge that all of creation, including nature, is alienated from what it should be. This alienation is called sin. It means that the thoughts and actions of human beings are directed inwardly toward self-aggrandizement. Sin is a manifestation of holding the self above others and above God. In this sense Christianity is not so different from Buddhism. Both traditions diagnose desire and self-serving as the cause of human alienation. Christianity says that, though we know what ought to be and how to do it, we are immersed in a condition that makes this virtually impossible. In Jesus, the teacher, and the son of humankind, God has shared the suffering of a world that lives in sin and alienation. By sharing that suffering to the death, he gives us hope. He shows us that suffering and death are overcome by the reign of God and not the reign of self. We have only to give up our self-centered posturings and let the love of God be the rule of our lives.

Now, I have greatly simplified Buddhism and Christianity in order to illustrate that religions exist as a means of contending with the fact *that people do bad things.* All great world religions have come into being *because* people do bad things. The human condition is, one way or another, the doing of bad things. Just because masses of people have identified themselves with these religions will not necessarily rid the world of the bad things that people do, sometimes in the *name* of religion. Sometimes, violence cannot be avoided even by some of the best representatives of a religion. Evil is complex; we are often responsible for evil we did not personally intend. A religion is authentic and worthy to the extent that it helps us understand and contend with this part of our existence. We could tell a similar story for all of the world's religions as well as for the beautiful traditions of nonliterate people such as Native Americans and tribal Africans. Religion serves to provide harmony for a life in which all kinds of chaos and discord are rampant.

Everything that human beings do is a reflection of the disharmony of existence. Since there is a gap between what ought to be and what is, and since people are constantly doing bad things *even when they intend otherwise,* our religions also may be used as instruments of desire or self-aggrandizement and may therefore bring suffering and sorrow. After all, my religion is a means of social and personal identity as well as a means of transformation. If my identity is threatened, I may entertain a great number of actions, some violent, in order to protect it. Or, simply by virtue of belonging to a certain group, I may be involved in violence I do not intend. It goes without saying that few, if any of us, can escape being agents of suffering. That is our condition. My religion should help me to see and understand that. It should help me to be an agent of enlightenment and love. It should help me to live creatively with my own complicity in the bad things people do, often in the name of religion.

There is a story from the tradition of the dervishes, those monkish figures in the Sufi movement of the Islamic world. It is one of the Nasrudin tales. Mullah Nasrudin was seated with a group of his followers, when one of them turned to him and asked, "What is the proper relationship between what ought to be and what is?"

Nasrudin replied, "You must be aware of the many levels on which we understand such matters."

"Show me something practical, Mullah," said the disciple, "something like an apple from Paradise so that I might see clearly what ought to be. Then I will be satisfied."

So Nasrudin picked up an apple and handed it to the man. "But this apple is rotten on one side. Certainly an apple from Paradise would be perfect."

"Perhaps," replied the Mullah, "but from where we sit in this habitation of evil and imperfection, and with your present perception, this is as close to a heavenly apple as you are likely to come."

We may have insights into what ought to be. We may live with a certain anxiety about the human inability to do what is best for the realm of nature as well as for ourselves. But even the most intelligent of our scientists and artists is a doer of evil and sees through a glass darkly. As Loren Eiseley has put it, "Reality has a way of hiding even from its most gifted observers." Our most gifted perceptions and most sincere intentions are likely to be as an apple that is rotten on one side, but this is as close to a heavenly apple as we are likely to get. According to Siddhartha, it is desire that accounts for suffering. In the Christian tradition it is sin, the alienation from God, that creates our dim perception of reality and a poor performance in the doing of good and right things. People do bad things in the name of their religions because they are prone to self-worship and desire. Yet it is religion that helps us understand our plight. Religion also provides the resources for serious disciples who wish to be open to a new dimension of behavior that transcends the inclination to do bad things, whether in the name of religion or not.

The Way of the Masses, the Way of Discipleship

Man, since the beginning of his symbol-making mind, has sought to read the map of [the] Universe. Do not believe those serious-minded men who tell us that writing began with economics and the ordering of jars of oil. Man is, in reality, an oracular animal. Bereft of instinct, he must search constantly for meanings. We forget that, like a child, man was a reader before he became a writer, a reader of what Coleridge once called the mighty alphabet of the universe.

With those words Loren Eiseley shares his message: that human beings have separated themselves from the realms of nature and as a result find it necessary to fashion a way of giving order and meaning to their existence. Inasmuch as we think of ourselves as *other* than nature, we find little meaning *in* nature. We conclude that life can only be meaningful if we can *fashion* something meaningful. Meaning and goodness will be the result of what *we* do. *We* must control the world that is other than ourselves, the world we call nature, and make of it something that satisfies our self-centered desires.

It is necessary for us to know who we are in the scheme of things. We must find self-identity, cultural identity. The search for identity is an expression of our religious need for ultimate order and meaning, but if we assume we are other than nature, then we will also conclude that our identity is somewhat separate from nature, something of our own choosing. Eiseley tells us that our search for meaning is a departure from instinct. Perhaps this is true, but after all, human instinct is not the same as animal instinct. For us, it is a natural affair that we should read the alphabet of the universe, that we should discover there the clues and symbols that fashion order and meaning for us.

It may be instinct that makes all of us religious, living with a distinctive view of the world that gives rise to our ideas, our ritualist life, and our sense of belonging. The way of the masses is an almost instinctive craving for, and confidence in, some such religious assurance. The way of the masses is not limited to the ignorant, uneducated, or nonintellectuals. It is not limited to the poor. This instinctive religiousness of the masses includes many affluent, intelligent, and educated persons. In some sense, it includes us all. The instinctive religiousness of the masses is not always a conscious religiosity, as we have seen. Many people are instinctively religious without being aware of it, without "practicing" a recognizable religion. Still others are instinctive practitioners of a specific religion; they use it, or find it significant, as a way of giving order and meaning to their lives. It is a means of hope, a pattern of consolation, a way of "being sure about things."

There is nothing inherently wrong with the instinctive way of the masses. We do not judge it out of court, for we are *all* of the masses. We are all instinctive readers and practitioners of Coleridge's "mighty alphabet of the universe." However, beneath the instinctive level on which our religiousness *ordinarily* operates, there is a special way—the way of discipleship. It is a way of special discipline, insight, knowledge, and wisdom. A way of enlightenment. If a disciple is faithful, he will be shocked out of his self-consciousness so that his perception is altered. He will have undergone enlightenment, and, presumably, he will become a servant of others rather than a person who seeks to control others. The way of discipleship is a path to *transformed* existence.

In his thirty-fifth year the light broke upon Siddhartha. In his thirtieth year the skies opened and the light fell upon Jesus: "Thou are my beloved Son." And the cave near Mt. Hira was the place of Muhammad's illumination in his fortieth year: "Recite!" In each case the present and ordinary perception was transformed. In each case there emerged a discovery of truth and a path for disciples to follow. For those who sought the way of discipleship there was a possibility of altered perception—of seeing and knowing beyond the ordinary.

It is also true that in each case there were masses of people who used the personality and insight of the Master (whether Siddartha, Jesus, or Muhammad) merely as a way of giving order and meaning to their lives. They had neither the time nor the inclination to be disciples. Yet they instinctively found the experiences of Siddhartha, Jesus, or Muhammad to be useful for giving meaning to their lives. They knew who they were.

They had some sense of what was real, what life was all about. They could hope and feel a certain assurance about the future. The masses converted the extraordinary perception of the master and his disciples into an instinctive way of giving order and meaning to their existence. Every religion is both a way of the masses as well as a way of discipleship. When we read statistics that inform us that there are millions of Muslims, Christians, Buddhists, Jews, and Hindus living in various parts of the planet, we must remember that the statistics refer to the way of the masses. We have no way of knowing the real number of those who pursue the way of discipleship.

During the lingering war between the nations of Iraq and Iran, we heard stories of boys who performed various kinds of suicide missions on behalf of their country. They were convinced there was a holiness to their actions, that they were guaranteed some distinction in a future existence. The lads performed willingly. From the perspective of most of us who live in the Western world, these actions were incomprehensible. To many of us those boys did evil to themselves and to others in the name of their religion. To many of us it was fanaticism, Islamic fanaticism. However, if we understand the instinctive necessity of humans to preserve a way that makes sense of *ordinary* existence, we begin to realize that some among the masses of people will do anything to protect or advance their particular world in its ordinances.

As I said in an earlier chapter, the "striving in the path of God" (jihad) is, *for the disciple*, a way of personal transformation; but for the masses it can become a basis for execution, terrorism, or crusade. The circumstances in which we find ourselves may frequently determine the manner in which we interpret our religious commitments. As part of the masses, we all require a significant measure of security and justification for our lives. If I feel fear, injustice, or inferiority, I may seek resolution in the texts, the teachings, or the simple identity provided by religion. The prayer of the rich man is often quite different from the prayer of the poor man. If I have not yet been introduced to the great transforming teaching at the heart of a religious tradition, as a member of the masses I will seek what I personally desire most. If I and my people have been patronized and exploited by another people, we may very well search our texts for some evidence that will allow us to believe that someday the exploiter will receive his just reward. I may even try to find a text that justifies my actions against the exploiter.

The way in which many Christians use the Bible exemplifies this kind of search for the satisfaction of personal desires. The reader of the Revelation of John (in the Christian New Testament) gets the distinct impression that the author has suffered so much persecution that he envisions a future in which the tables will be turned, and those who persecuted will be in eternal misery. He seeks vengeance. Popular belief in heaven and hell is a form of projected violence in the name of religion.

Religion, as a way of the masses, always includes a variety of social, economic, and political factors. As we study the world's religions we discover that many of them will develop special teachings that are designed to justify certain acts of violence. Violence is frequently justified when the way of the masses is threatened.

You as a Christian, and I as a Muslim, may live in relative harmony with each other. I inhabit a world in which everything I think and do is informed by the Koran and the traditions of my people. As a Muslim my economics, politics, and social order (my sense of interpersonal relationships) are all formed by the way of Islam. Life is given order and meaning by Islamic tradition. This is a total world I inhabit. If for any reason you begin to threaten the truth of my world, I must be able to justify protecting it. You may threaten the order and meaning of my world in an economic way, a political way, or simply by insulting my basic convictions. In any case, it is a religious threat. The way in which masses of people live, the very world in which they exist, becomes vulnerable. It must be defended and this defense may take the form of a jihad, a crusade, a holy war.

In the sixth century C.E. the emperor of Japan received a gift of a gold-plated image of Buddha, along with some sacred writings and a letter advocating the learning of Buddhist doctrine. The emperor was impressed by the news that this teaching had found acceptance in the lands of India, China, and Korea. He discussed the matter with his advisers and decided the doctrine should be given a chance. However, there were many who feared that the native gods of Japan, the kami, would be angered by such a threat to their world. When disease, such as plague, began to ravage the people, it was taken as evidence of the displeasure of the kami. The golden image of Buddha was thrown into a canal and Buddhism was abandoned.

The masses live in a tidy world. Everything fits. Everything has its place. Matters of cause and effect are easily understood by the people.

For the masses of Japanese, including many of the learned people, the kami closely regulated the realms of nature and human conduct. Any evidence of ill-fated hardship or disaster was due to the kami's displeasure. The gods demanded that alien forces and ideas be eliminated. We may not condone whatever evil the emperor or the people may have done in the name of their religion, but we should be able to understand that the way of the masses is a law-and-order world where everything fits neatly into place. The causes of evil and suffering are readily identified and handled.

In recent years we have had many reports from India about the strained relationships between Hindus and Sikhs, Hindus and Muslims. There have been riots between these religious groups. Violence has caused death and injury, and starvation—all of it, in some sense, in the name of religion. The way of the masses led many Hindus into violent actions. For many Hindus the importance of their religion as a means of providing social identity and worldview justified whatever action was necessary to defend their world.

However, there is in the Hindu tradition a way of discipleship as well as a way of the masses. Mahatma Gandhi was a Hindu who believed God is the *only* reality, the only real Truth. Much of life is spent trying to pretend this is not so. We prefer not to live with the truth; instead, we prefer to live with the illusion that what we ordinarily know is truth, that we ourselves are real. Yet only God is real. Only truth is real, and the right way to live is to search for it.

The evils of this world are the result of holding on to the illusion that *I* am real, *I* am truth—that my way and my selfhood are real. Good is served by rejecting that illusion and searching for the only Truth there is. "For me," said Gandhi, "the only certain means of knowing God is nonviolence." What he meant was a renunciation of the will to kill or injure, for whatever reason. To be willing to murder or damage another living being was to permit the illusion of separate selfhood to continue. Violence is generated by the refusal to allow only God to be real. Mahatma Gandhi had examined the literature and traditions of India's religions. He had investigated the way of the masses and found deep within it a way of discipleship. Following the way of discipleship opened up the possibility of a transformed existence. Gandhi discovered that he ceased to hate anyone and could do violence to no one. The inner violence that leads to violent action was gone.

The way of discipleship, which is at the heart of all the major religious traditions of the world, has a potential for disclosing a mode of personal transformation that rises above violence. Mahatma Gandhi's discovery of Truth did not blind him to the fact that human beings were being exploited by the British in India and by the Hindu caste system. To continue to tolerate these evil systems would have permitted injustice to be prolonged. Such toleration demonstrated no real love for the persons who defended the evil systems. Toleration only condoned the illusions under which they lived.

Gandhi recognized an apparent dilemma. The British in India were doing violence by way of their colonial system. Masses for whom Hinduism provided an understanding of their place in the world were also doing bad things in the name of religion through adherence to a caste system and resistance to British rule. Yet the disciple, whose life is transformed, does not hate even his enemy and cannot be drawn into violent action. What was to be done to oppose the violence, while showing love for those who were responsible for it? Gandhi's answer was nonviolent but active resistance—noncooperation with the work of the evil system. The disciple is willing to suffer, even die in the course of this kind of nonviolent resistance. After all, his death is not the death of a self, but a further journey into the one true reality that is God. "No country has ever risen without being purified through the fire of suffering," wrote Gandhi. "Life comes out of Death. Will India rise out of her slavery without fulfilling this eternal law of purification through suffering?" In a great measure, Gandhi was responsible for the independence of India and for radical changes in the culture and politics of his native land. He suffered and died in the course of nonviolent action against tyranny.

It is not my purpose in this chapter to be an apologist, a defender of the life and work of Mahatma Gandhi. His story stands out, however, as an illustration of my basic point: that every religion is both a way of the masses and a way of discipleship; that the way of discipleship generally leads to transformed living that avoids violence. But the way of the masses is also essential, because no people can exist outside a world of ultimate order and meaning.

What of the fanatic? Isn't the fanatic an extremely dedicated and devout disciple? Americans as a rule tend to deemphasize the depth of their commitment to religion because they are fearful of being called fanatics. "My wife is a fanatic," say many American males, smug in a kind of forced machismo, "She goes to church whenever the doors open. And she's always reading religious stuff. Me? Well, I believe in God and all that, but you gotta live in this world. I'm not *that* religious. Not a fanatic."

In most instances, if we really investigated the life of such a person, described by her husband as a fanatic, we would probably encounter someone who simply takes her religious potential seriously. She would hardly be a fanatic, if by fanatic we mean someone whose zeal is unreasonable or destructive. Fortunately we have a model for our understanding of fanaticism in this stage of history. The image of the Ayatollah Khomeini of Iran loomed before us as one whose religious zeal is destructive. Of course, we did not know the Ayatollah. We only knew what television cameras, photographers, and the news media revealed to us. Perhaps their revelation did violence to the Ayatollah. What the media gave us was the *image* of a fanatic. We must remember he was human flesh as we are; that he had the same needs, committed similar errors, and occasionally did a good deed. It may be true that he was a fanatic, a person who persistently did bad things in the name of religion, but every fanatic provides us with excuses for avoiding the responsibility of developing the human dignity, personal freedom, and growth, that lie at the heart of our religious nature. When we hear about the bad deeds of a fanatic, we say, "See? I told you. This is what religious people are like. This is what happens when you fool around with religion."

This is an irresponsible comment that shows little understanding of religion or human nature. Religion is the one thing intelligent people should earnestly study; yet it is the most neglected of studies. The comment is itself a fanatically religious comment by someone who doesn't realize how zealous he is about defending his world and how unreasonable he is in not recognizing the image of the Ayatollah in himself.

It is difficult to define fanaticism. In a *literal* sense the woman whose husband describes her as one who "goes to church whenever the doors are open" really is a fanatic. The word *literally* refers to someone who frequents the *fanum,* the temple. But words often go beyond their literal or original meanings, and for us a fanatic is a destructively zealous person, not merely one who frequents the temple. The question before us is whether the fanatic and the disciple are one and the same.

We might well ask, Was Gandhi a fanatic? Martin Luther King? Francis of Assisi? Jesus of Nazareth? Siddhartha Gautama? Generally speaking, we would not consider these persons fanatical. Perhaps that is primarily *because* they did *not* do bad things in the name of religion. Yet they were deeply representative of their religion. They were disciples. Their devotion and commitment resulted in transformed ways of life that were not destructive. They were exponents of love and justice whose lives embodied the quality of reconciliation.

Fanatics are seldom representatives of the way of discipleship. Instead they are defenders of the way of the masses. The Ayatollah Khomeini or Rabbi Meir Kahane of the Jewish Defense League did not act and speak from the depths of their traditions. They apparently did not have their lives transformed by a disciplined centering of their existence. The disciple is constantly aware that his own life is not what it ought to be, that he participates in a world that is not what it should be (see the previous chapter). He has learned from the tradition that this distortion of existence is the result of a self that is centered upon its own desires, and that the distortion affects the way we perceive other persons and creatures of this world.

The disciple learns from the tradition he follows that it is possible to re-center existence. The tradition teaches him that transformed perception, transformed existence is possible. Thus the disciple is unlikely ever to be a fanatic, a zealous defender of a worldview. He may have to fight the temptation to be a zealot, but he fights it with an energy that is not his own. He becomes ever more as Gandhi was when he discovered he did not hate anyone even though he saw the injustice and the violence of governments and systems.

The zealot or fanatic, on the other hand, is concerned with defending the identity and sense of social solidarity that the way of the masses provides. He does not wish to see his Protestant world collapse under the threat of Catholicism or Communism. He is anxious that his Islamic beliefs and values may be compromised by a Christian world that is becoming increasingly technological and secularized. He worries that the Sikhs may be absorbed and assimilated into the larger Hindu culture. He begins to sabotage, to conspire, and to fight this enemy of *his world*. The fanatic's religiousness seldom moves beyond its concern for the preservation of the way of the masses. It is satisfied with its ordinary perception of the world. It wants no more from religion than assurance that the world is rightly and meaningfully ordered.

The outsider, a person who identifies with no religious tradition, has little consolation that he does not consciously do bad things in the name of some religion. For, as we have already seen, he does not escape his religious nature, and he will quickly assume a religious stance with regard to some social, political, or intellectual movement. He may even become so anxious about it that he is willing to do violence for its preservation.

The way of the disciple is the way out of violence. In a recent adult class on the importance of storytelling, I was discussing the need for each of us to be able to tell his or her own story. Every person's story is an account of a private, social, and cosmic self. Yet all three of these aspects of your story and mine are intricately related. As soon as I begin to tell the secret parts of my story, I discover that they have to do with other people, other things and ideas, and finally, with a sense of what it all means—how it all fits together as a whole. As soon as I begin to tell my story, I discover that it always involves others and is never ending. The more seriously I take this business of storytelling, the more I become a pilgrim inside my own tale. I become a person who has been touched by the truth of my own story, and I am drawn to search for a more complete vision of that truth. It is at this stage that the stories that are part of religious traditions become meaningful. The story of religion renders my own story more complete and meaningful.

Siddhartha Gautama's Hindu culture was part of his private story, but it was not until he began to come to terms with his story that the special story of enlightenment broke into his consciousness. The story of good news, the Gospel of Christianity, will make little sense to anyone who first has not begun to tell his own story. Thus much contemporary preaching in American churches tends to be little more than ineffective incantation. Unless the preacher helps you tell your story in such a way that you see the significance of everyday events as part of the need to find order and meaning, it will do little good for him or her to recite words about salvation and reconciliation. People will be content with the order and meaning their culture already shares with them. They will be content with the way of the masses. The possibility of discipleship is opened up only for those who, in coming to terms with their own stories, begin to see the relevance of the stories that are called religions.

Buddhism is a story that has profound insights to contribute to your storytelling. Christianity is the story of God's sharing in the human drama of success and failure, good and evil, sorrow and joy. It is the story of God's triumph over our alienation from each other and from the foundation of being, God himself. Christianity is the story of suffering and triumph, the story of God being human so that humanity may be nearer to God. Discovering the power of the Buddhist story may lead the individual into a way of discipleship that results in enlightenment. Discovering the power of the Christian story may lead the disciple into the way of the transformed mind, wherein he discovers that he is involved in making things whole. Hence the disciple overcomes his natural inclination to do violence. Rather, he does not overcome it, but perceives that it is overcome and that his life rejects violence, often in spite of himself. He does not cease to struggle with the natural and ordinary inclination, but the struggle that takes place is part of a story in which violence is overcome, in which life is victorious over death.

Martin Luther King, Jr. was a striking example of the point I am making. Americans recognize him as a leader in the twentieth-century struggle to achieve full citizenship for African Americans. King did not hate white Americans, but he had learned that unjust and evil systems cannot be tolerated. Injustice must be resisted by those who are willing to suffer on behalf of others. He accepted suffering not merely in order to achieve freedom and justice for blacks, but also to expose the true character of the oppressors, for oppression prevents the oppressor from being fully human. The oppressor must be resisted for his own benefit, but it does no good to do violence to him. Violence feeds upon its own heroics and turns the liberator into a tyrant.

Violence breeds violence. Not only does it do harm to the other person, it encourages the violence already present in him. Oppressed people are nurtured on violence, and the violence waits inside, often unrecognized, for the tables to be turned. Unless the oppressed person has a way of restraining or converting that violence, it will find expression whenever the opportunity is provided. The terrorist is often a person who has known the effects of violence. Because the violence was inflicted by those who represented a different religion, the terrorist will direct his own violence at the representatives of that religion on behalf of his own. Thus bad things are done in the name of religion when it remains only the way of the masses. The way of the masses is so concerned with maintaining the order and meaning of the world that it justifies violence.

Martin Luther King, Jr. was a disciple. He had discovered that the story of his life was informed by other stories that possessed a certain power of transformation. At its heart the Christian story is the way of the disciple, even though it has become a way of the masses for many throughout history. That story was central to King's life as he reflected on the story of African-American captivity and the story of another disciple, Mohandas Gandhi. If one became a disciplined follower and probed the depth of these stories, it would be possible to receive a new power of thought and action. "We shall match your capacity to inflict suffering," he wrote, "by our capacity to endure suffering. We will meet your physical force with soul-force."

King's "soul-force" was not a sentimental avoidance of evil and oppression. It was an enlightened understanding that the violence in our lives cannot be resisted by ordinary efforts or good intentions. We must learn to see our own violence in the eyes of another who may be our oppressor. We resist violence in ourselves and in others with a power that is not of our own design. The struggle for justice in an unjust world is a power struggle, but the power for the disciple is a soul-force, not a physical force.

Often when we turn to the ancient religions, before the time of Siddhartha, Jesus, and Plato, we discover a way of the masses filled with stories of war gods and bloody sacrifices. Of course, it is easy for us to dismiss such stories as evidence of primitive immorality, ignorance, and bloodthirstiness. There is no time or space here to interpret the ancients, to show how and why they were not so unenlightened as we judge them to be. What some of these stories and practices suggest, however, is that there is a surface meaning that reflects the way of the masses even as there is a deeper meaning that is discerned by the disciple who is prepared to ask questions. The masses may be satisfied with the violence, indeed may wish to defend its necessity and maintain it as a way of order and meaning in religion. The disciple knows that the stories of the gods contain a secret about life—a secret that is gradually revealed to one who perseveres.

From the epic Avesta, the sacred tradition and scriptures of Zoroastrianism, this story emerges. Thousands of years ago in the time when the Aryans of Iran and the Aryans of India lived side by side in their original homeland, there lived a great chief who was a sage. He was also a physician and a priest who performed the Haoma (Soma) ritual of preparing and drinking the intoxicating juice of a special plant. The Haoma was pleased and so the chief was granted two sons.

One son became a judge and lawgiver. However, he was a strict interpreter of the law and there were those who objected to his judgments. One day he was murdered by Hitaspa the Crowned, a prince who did not like this rigid man of the law.

The second son was named Keresaspa and he became a warrior. He was called the manly minded, the long-haired one who carried a heavy, spiked mace. Keresaspa ascended the golden throne of his father and pledged to avenge the death of his brother. He rode on his chariot to a river bank and invoked the wind god, praying with consecrated twigs and milk that he might be victorious. The mace of Keresaspa crushed the skull of Hitaspa, whose dead body was tied to the chariot.

There are many tales of Keresaspa's exploits. He slew a huge yellow dragon that haunted the forests and devoured men and horses. There was Gandarewa the Golden-Heels, a pirate who raided ships and coastal villages. Sea trade was a risky business with this man on the loose. Many a hero had been his victim. Keresaspa sacrificed a hundred horses, a thousand bulls, and ten thousand rams to the water deity. In this grand ritual feast he invoked the god to grant him victory over Gandarewa. Then on a stormy day along the coast the two met in violent combat. In the end the pirate's corpse lay on the shore, washed by the waves.

Snavidhka was a boastful lad with an iron fist. With one stroke he could slay a man. He went around punching poor people. "I am still a boy," he would shout. "When I become a man I will turn the earth into a wheel and the sky into a chariot. Then I will pull the Good Spirit down from heaven and the Evil Spirit up from hell and tie them to my chariot!" Keresaspa, the long-haired, shut this blasphemer's mouth forever.

The gods were pleased with Keresaspa. He lived long and brought security, peace, and prosperity to his people. But he fell in love with a beautiful witch, Khanaiti. She cast a spell that would make him forget the good deeds he had done and the values for which he stood. And so one day he fell into a deep sleep and never awoke. His body still awaits the day of resurrection.

This story is filled with violence and vengeance. The gods come to the aid of the hero, in order that he might slay evildoers. One could use the story to say that the gods are defenders of our people, our way of life, our worldview. They help us eliminate our enemies. It seems to be quite normal, even natural, for us to assume that Keresaspa knew how to manipulate the gods to his own ends, which, of course, are considered just and righteous. Whether we are traditionally religious or not, our religiousness identifies with Keresaspa. He represents the kind of world we desire. He is on the right side, which, in our thinking, is always *our* side.

The humanist or scientist who looks out on a world of ignorance and violence assumes he is Keresaspa. He could readily go to war against the stupidity and cruelty that threaten his sense of order and meaning. This might be contrary to the best principles of science and humanistic learning because those principles demand that we accept our own ignorance and cruelty. They require us to see the unknown in the midst of the known, to see the mystery that is at the heart of all knowledge. Yet most of us forget that mystery. We prefer the order and meaning that are immediately present and meet our demands. He who sees the mystery is a disciple, even though he be a scientist or humanistic scholar. He who demands an order to life that readily identifies the ignorant evildoer exercises his religiousness only as a way of the masses.

For many of us, the story of Keresaspa is either a proof that the religious mind leads to violence, or it is a story that helps us to justify our own violent actions against evildoers. However, would it not be possible that such a story is for disciples and not for ordinary religious minds? When the disciple hears the story, he discovers he is all of the characters in the story, not just one. He learns that wisdom is the gift of recognizing a balance between the lawgiver and the hero. The strict lawgiver invites violence, perhaps his own demise. The hero in us, who attempts to avenge injustice, does battle with forces of nature and with the arrogant side of us that assumes that we can control all things—even good and evil, God and the Evil One. Then, too, we are easily seduced at every stage of our existence, particularly in time of great accomplishment and personal satisfaction. The hero is easy prey to seduction, because he assumes he is only a hero. But he is really all of the characters. When he discovers that, he is enlightened. He awakens in resurrection, out of the death of his seduction.

Khanaiti was beautiful, and it is easy to give ourselves to one who promises all that we desire. But desire leads to suffering, to enslavement. The wise person is the disciple who learns that desire can only be transcended, never satisfied. If desire leads us to the mystery of existence, it is good. If it leads us to suspect that we can get whatever we want, it will lead to evil.

I have tried in this chapter to suggest that every religious tradition is to some extent a way of the masses and a way of discipleship. Not everyone who is satisfied with the way of the masses will be a purveyor of violence. Perhaps there are also times when the disciple will find himself without enough grace to raise himself above his involvement in evil. However, the disciple is generally concerned with more than maintaining the simple order and meaning of his world. He knows there is a special knowledge and a special power at the heart of existence, that religious tradition is the teacher of that knowledge and power, and that these are the antithesis of violence. The disciple is not as likely to be involved in violence in the name of religion.

It is important to understand that our religiousness functions in this same manner whether or not we are loyal to a particular religion. The most sophisticated of humans as well as the most deprived of us tend to respond to life either as disciples in search of the mystery or as defenders of the way of the masses. It does no good to blame religions for the bad things of this world. We are all characters in the story of Keresaspa.

The Demon
of the Absolute

I never believed in demons until I began reading the stories of Isaac Bashevis Singer. At first I didn't know what to make of his stories. They were so different from much of the literature of our times. I suspect many potential readers may be put off by an initial encounter with his work. There are some unfamiliar terms, and the tales come out of the great memory of orthodox Jewry. They are filled with all kinds of mysterious happenings: miracles, dead corpses dancing, obsessive love, curious sexual behavior somehow linked to the life of the Holy One. Strange events. Tormented souls. At first I was intimidated by Singer's crazy world, so different from a sane technological world. I laid the books aside. Who could fathom such superstitious goings-on? Without a very specialized vocabulary and a taste for the vanished, the antiquated, and extinct, it seemed impossible to enjoy these stories.

I can't remember what changed my mind. It could have had something to do with the fact that I played the role of Tevye in a musical-theatre production of *Fiddler on the Roof*. All these circumstances seem to have been concentrated at a certain period of my life, but the point is that I found myself reading Singer with an intense fascination: I had discovered a master storyteller. I was initiated into an astonishing world in which things were real that had previously been either vague assumptions or else quaint remnants or an unenlightened age. I began to accept the presence of those demons and dybbuks that inhabit the world Singer describes.

You don't believe in demons? Never you mind. They don't need you to believe in them. They are not like God. It's not a matter of belief! It's a matter of sight. Look in a mirror! There is bound to be an imp on your shoulder, though he will disappear as quickly as you realize his presence.

The demon is there if you can see him; you only have to be initiated into a world where such seeing is a rather ordinary affair. "There is a kind of net that is as old as Methuselah," says one of these creatures in Singer's story "The Mirror," "as soft as a cobweb and as full of holes, yet it has retained its strength to this day. When a demon wearies of chasing after yesterdays or going round in circles on a windmill, he can install himself inside a mirror. There he waits like a spider in its web, and the fly is certain to be caught."

After all, says Singer, we lived for thousands of years and knew nothing about germs. Who could believe in a germ? What is so unusual about demons when people have been aware of them for a long time? I saw these demons in action in Singer's stories where they were frequently central characters. The story could not have been told without them. Of course, demons "like overcast skies [and] old houses." Isaac Singer doesn't think it would be easy to find demons in the Promised Land. "The climate is too beautiful," he says, "and there is so much sunshine I think they would have great difficulty in Israel." Perhaps in Safed, that town in the mountains where the kabbalists used to live, there they might be at home. The only trouble is that there is a population of angels in Safed, Singer reminds us, and demons would not like that.

I think Isaac Singer may be wrong about Israel. I think there are lots of demons there. So much history. In Jerusalem I think they are very numerous—in old walls, old streets, tombs, churches, and mosques. Demons are like church mice; they enjoy such places. I think they also like the challenge of angels. So many battles have been fought in Israel. Assassinations, massacres, crucifixions, and so much holiness and praying—even a resurrection: if there are demons anywhere, they would certainly inhabit such sites.

Yes, I think there are demons there in spite of the sunshine. Where there is much love and devotion, there is often much hate; and hate is caused by the playfulness, the practical jokes, and the devious ugliness of imps and demons. "But there is one demon," writes Paul Elmer More, "who retains so much celestial glamour, and so wears the robe of authority, that he still moves about unnoticed or passes for an angel of light. And the mischief of his art is that the finer minds are often those most subject to his wiles. I mean the Demon of the Absolute."

How can it be that the absolute is called a demon? In my classes at the university I try to teach students what I call historical perspective. This is the ability to see that all things exist in relationship to all sorts of "others"—other things, ideas, persons, and beings. The notions of past, present, and future are artificial. They are human conveniences. History is therefore not really a study of the past. It is way of looking, of seeing. It is a perspective. History is a way of telling the story of relationships in time and space. That may be a concept too difficult to explain in the brief confines of this chapter, but that is what I try to teach. Perhaps I should say it is the *way* I try to teach. At any rate, it tends to make some people nervous, and so I am frequently visited by a student who wants to know whether I believe in the absolute. I ask her why she wants to know.

Almost without fail, the student launches into a long discourse on why absolutes are necessary. Someone who doesn't believe in absolutes also doesn't believe in God, she will tell me. It is essential to have absolutes or the world will collapse. When I look up from my desk, I usually see a curious little creature sitting on the shoulder of the anxious student. He is a nervous little one, but he is still giggling to his heart's delight, and he is whispering all kinds of threatening things. Such a demon as this sits on the shoulder of people who become fanatics, crusaders, fundamentalists. He makes them nervous, so nervous they sometimes do very bad things as a testimony to the abolute. They act as protectors of the absolute, even though it is rather absurd to imagine that the absolute should require protection.

It is rather easy to observe that the demon on the shoulder of the erstwhile defender of the absolute is a servant of desire. Recall how Siddhartha discovered that desire is the second "Noble Truth" and the cause of suffering. Recall how the Nazarene learned that desire is the way in which the self seeks to remain at the center of existence? Desire separates us from God. Desire is sin. The student becomes nervous because she sees the grand object of the self's desire disappearing. Most absolutes are forms of the self projected onto a very large screen. People might fear the loss of the absolute because it represents the collapse of the way they desire things to be.

The absolute is that upon which no conditions can be put. Of almost everything in life it is possible to chart changes. Persons and things always exist with limitations, conditions. Conditions in my life determine my health, my physical and mental well-being. They set the tone of how well I behave and what I will achieve. Conditions are the result of the existence of other beings, to whom I am related in some way. Existence is conditioned by relationships. Needless to say, it is very uncomfortable for me to admit that. Therefore I will project this dissatisfaction onto a large screen that pictures the Absolute. When I speak of the Absolute I am usually thinking of a self that exists without limitations. If I cry out for absolute values, I am usually seeking to justify my shaky self-image. I will fight to protect the Absolute because I am struggling to overcome my limitations, the conditions in which my life is set.

Does this mean there is nothing that exists without conditions? The only truth without condition is that existence is conditioned by relationships. All of this sounds very abstract and philosophical, but the sense of it is really quite simple: the one absolute is that no one's understanding of the truth is the whole truth. Whatever truth we see is always seen in relationship to something. The one absolute truth seems to be that no absolute is really what we say it is. What we suggest to be absolute is always what is seen and thought by our limited perception. When some of the great Asian traditions speak of the Absolute, they are really referring to that *absence*, that emptiness, that calls all so-called absolutes into question. It is of the nature of the Absolute that it can condone no absolutes. It rejects them as demons.

One of the great theoretical scientists of this century was the German Werner Heisenberg, and one of his most profound insights is that all scientific observation is influenced by the *instrument* that is used to make the observation. This means that what is observed is limited: it is conditioned by the instruments of observation. If I look at something with a microscope the microscope is a factor in what I see. What I observed is not absolute—it is not without conditions. Since all instruments of observation are in some sense the product of inquiring *minds*, it may be suggested that our reasoning minds are also instruments of observation. Therefore, our minds influence the results of their reasoning. They cannot arrive at absolute truths, only truths that are the legacy of their own limited search.

The great religious traditions of the world have understood this principle. Ofttimes scientists forget it and practitioners of religion forget it because people like absolutes. They like to fight for absolutes. It is inconvenient for them to believe that the only real absolute is that we are not to be trusted with absolutes. When the Muslim recites the Shahada, he says, "There is no god except Allah." This means that there is no god but "*the* God"—A'llah. For some Muslims this probably means "I have a god who is better than any other god. He is really *the* God, the Absolute!" Of course, if he tells me that, I will want to reply to him,

"My God is just as absolute as yours. Perhaps more so!" We may fight about it. We may have so-called Muslim fundamentalists fighting with followers of conservative American morality, each group in defense of an absolute, and the demon will sit on their shoulders as they fight. He will be laughing, victorious again. When the truth of the Koran was revealed to Muhammad—there is no god but *the* God—it was a discovery that people are always creating gods that are extensions of their minds as instruments of desire and observations. They are creating absolutes. Muhammad learned that there is *no god,* no absolute. You must always refuse to worship your absolutes. That is the real truth of Allah, the God.

Muhammad discovered what had also been revealed to Moses—"thou shalt have *no other gods* before me." The only absolute is that there are no absolutes. Life is always an affair of "no other gods," please! I know that my desiring mind is always a factor in what it learns and concludes. Therefore, it cannot know an absolute. I know only that there is in my mind the wisdom to know there is no absolute. The mind is more than it seems to be. There can be no other god before it because mind is part of God, though never all of God.

The Christian tradition takes seriously what Heisenberg concluded. If it is true that what I observe is the consequence of my relationship to what I am observing, then the *relationship* itself is very important. It means that I know the truth in terms of my relationship to it. That is why Christianity emphasizes what is called the doctrine of incarnation. Incarnation is embodiment: God is God-with-us. God is in-relationship. He is not the absolute of our reasoning desire. When the Christian encounters Jesus Christ he is witness to a life that seems to say, "Ah! Your careful definitions of God, the absolute, are too presumptuous; you must see that you only know God-with-us, whom you will probably kill on behalf of your absolute."

That the only absolute is that there are no absolutes is a very personal discovery. The truth is known in relationships. "Lex orandi, lex credendi" says an old proverb, which means that the rule of prayer (which is essentially a matter of relationship) is prior to the rule of understanding. "When you pray, don't theologize" is another adage.

Siddhartha learned that desire creates absolutes. The key to enlightened existence is to eliminate desire and thereby to move beyond all gods, all absolutes. The goal is Nirvana, the stream of being that is beyond our thinking, our expectations and attachments. Buddhist tradition tells us that before Siddhartha Gautama received enlightenment he was visited by the Evil One in the person of Mara, god of desire and death. "Why bother with this strange quest of yours, Siddhartha?" asked the tempter. "You will never find the answer. Settle for what you have, what you can get. You have earned it; that is truth enough."

Suddenly there appeared three beautiful, sensuous women accompanied by a retinue of erotic dancers. Gautama resisted, whereupon a host of demons appeared. They were terrifying, threatening him with wind and rain, attacking him with boiling mud, live coals, uprooted trees, glowing rocks, and fiery ashes. He who was to become Buddha, the Enlightened One, was unmoved. The Evil One and his demons had failed to convince him of the absolute power of such things as sexual pleasure and even the threats of personal destruction. Siddhartha saw the threat of death as a further attempt to delude him about the importance of the self. The great desire for the service and survival of the self creates absolutes. It would seem, on rational examination, that pleasure and self-survival are perfectly legitimate loyalties. After all, what is wrong with enjoying our bodies and protecting them? That is the initial question asked by the demon of the absolute. The demon is a master of logic.

Siddhartha's story is similar to the one about Jesus of Nazareth and his forty days in the wilderness after his baptism by John. Jesus, too, faces the demon of the absolute. After all, what is wrong with bread, wealth, and political power, or with certain evidence of unusual gifts that might be called magical or miraculous? Jesus resists the logic. "The Demon of the Absolute," wrote Paul Elmer More, "is nothing else but rationalism." It is "reason run amuck." Reason exists to help us make sense out of the actual circumstances of life. It is a guide, friend, and "without it we can do nothing wisely." But reason seeks to place the egoic self in the center of existence. It therefore creates absolutes out of what it observes. As More says, "There are no absolutes in nature; they are phantoms created by reason itself in its own likeness, delusions which, when once evoked, usurp the field of reality and bring endless confusion in their train."

It is this response of human reason to the demon of the absolute that is responsible for much of the violence in the world. People frequently do bad things in the name of religion because they have taken a phantom of reason and fashioned it into an absolute. Because our religious nature is eager to find security, it wishes to rest in a world where everything is carefully ordered and meaningful; it is always subject to the temptation of the Demon. The Demon says to reason, "What is wrong with you?

Here you are, all ready to be god and too shy to put on the robes. Is there not an Almighty, a Big Boss, in your head? Make that Almighty into the emperor of the universe. Then serve him well. And do not let anyone challenge his authority."

One of the most tyrannical of absolutes created by the religious and reasoning egoic self is the authoritarian God. There are masses of people in all parts of the world who have lived as servants of this tyrant. Servants of the tyrant find it easy to be tyrants themselves. Or else they find it expedient to use the tyrant to justify their violent actions against enemies in crusades and revolutions. Muhammad, after his unique discovery that there is no god but the God, found it difficult to live with that revelation among a people who wanted justification for action against their enemies. Soon the Demon of the Absolute created an authoritarian god who was powerful enough to make all other gods seem ungodlike. Soon this absolute god called for just and holy wars against those who would not recognize his authority.

To say there is no god but God is to understand that there are no absolutes. There is only the absolute truth that calls into question any opinion or action that sets itself up as justification for violence. For me to know that there are no absolutes, I must become increasingly aware of the manner in which my own person is involved in the discovery of this truth. Religious tradition helps me develop that awareness through its sense of gratitude and humility. The only absolute is a very *personal* sensitivity to the fact that there are no absolutes. The source of all being is present in our observing, thinking personalities; it is present as more than those personalities can comprehend.

Until we discover this truth, God tends to remain an Absolute outside our observing, thinking personalities. In other words, He is a kind of grand object created by us and assumed to be a whimsical creator, a tyrant over all he surveys. Such a God creates trouble. We have to be able to explain how He can be a good and merciful absolute and still permit all the suffering in our world. There are many ways to try to make that explanation. We can say God punishes us for our misdeeds as a loving parent does, although it is often difficult to see how the punishments fit the crimes. Were the Jews really such unfaithful servants of God that He could justify using the Nazis to exterminate six million of them?

The point here is that the God who is Absolute Other has been the supposed mastermind behind many of the bad things that have been done in the name of religion. Although the best of us continue to do bad things, many of us are tired of giving in to the Demon of the Absolute; and others of us who have become religiously indifferent have done so because we have set up this straw God of the Absolute and then proceeded to say we can no longer believe in God because we cannot understand how such an Absolute could allow terrible things to happen. These attitudes, however intelligent they may seem, belong to the way of the masses discussed in the previous chapter. If we would begin to ask the questions of a disciple who seeks to understand, to gain wisdom and enlightenment, we would discover that the great traditions are not representatives of the Absolute. Instead the wise persons of these traditions have learned that the real, personal, vital, and absolute truth is that there are no absolutes.

Early in the development of the Hebrew tradition, out of which the traditions of Judaism and Christianity emerged, there were those who thought Moses had been visited by the Absolute Other, He who called into question the power of all other gods. Actually it was the Demon of the Absolute who came and said to them, "Look! These other nations have made you suffer. They have imprisoned you, raped your women, and taken your children as slaves. They have massacred you, all in the name of their gods. But I speak to you as the Omnipotent One. I am the Absolute. I have chosen you to represent me. Together we shall avenge all the evil done against you!"

Not all of the Hebrews gave in to the Demon of the Absolute. They were not all worshipers of the God of revenge who justified terrible actions. There were those who understood what Abraham perceived: "I will make you a great nation and *through you all the people of the earth shall be blessed.*" The ancient writer knew that the true absolute was the knowledge that the truth is only found in relationships among the persons and other beings of the universe. There are no absolutes, only the good of all being. To forget that is to permit the earth to be destroyed.

This truth always disturbs the followers of the Absolute, who rules over all people with an iron hand as the representative of our demonic egos. In the second half of the Book of Isaiah, we discover the image of the absolute truth that there are no absolutes. The author speaks of one who "bore the sin of many and interceded for their transgressions." Force is renounced because God is no longer the Omnipotent Absolute but the Suffering Servant. God is known in suffering. In other words, He is the loving truth that is discovered in the midst of our foolish attempts to serve one absolute or another.

There is never any hope for a world that serves absolutes. Such service can only lead to violence. There is no victory, only hatred and revenge. The only genuine hope is in our response to human suffering. You can whip me into submission, but there will be no advancement of the human story in your success. I will either become vengeful and serve the righteousness of my absolute claim against you, or I will accept the suffering knowing that neither your god nor mine is really absolute. In the latter case, there is hope. In the former, there is none. God is the discovery in the midst of suffering that there are no absolutes.

There is a much-used passage from the writings of Elie Wiesel that illustrates this point. *The Night* tells of Wiesel's experience with the death camps and the Nazi extermination of Jewish people. "Why should I bless the Eternal?" he asked.

> Because He had thousands of children burned in His pits? Because He kept six crematories working night and day, on Sundays and feast days? Because in His great might He had created Auschwitz, Birkenau, Buna, and so many factories of death? How could I say to Him, "Blessed art thou, Eternal, Master of the Universe, who chose us from among the races to be tortured day and night, to see our fathers, our mothers, our brothers end in the crematory? Praised be Thy Holy Name, Thou who hast chosen us to be butchered on Thine altar?"

This was a young man who accused the Almighty, the Absolute, of misrepresentation. "I had ceased to be anything but ashes, yet I felt myself to be stronger than the Almighty." There is little doubt that the Holocaust, the slaughter of the Jews, is a profound indictment of the Absolute God. It is difficult to give loyalty to such a god in the wake of that agony.

But there was another observation to make. Elie Wiesel was witness to a hanging. Three people were to be executed by the SS. One of the three was a boy with a refined and beautiful face, loved by all in the camp. The three victims mounted the chairs beneath the gallows. Their heads were placed in nooses. At a sign from the commandant, the chairs were tipped over. The two adults died almost immediately, their tongues hanging swollen. However, for more than half an hour, the third rope still moved as the child struggled between life and death. The inmates marched past the third horrid sight. They witnessed his cruel death, tongue red, and the eyes not yet glazed. Behind Wiesel a man asked, "Where is God now?" "And I heard a voice within me answer him: 'Where is He? Here He is—He is hanging here on this gallows.' . . . "

Wiesel probably meant that God died there on that gallows—the existence of any Almighty, omnipotent, or absolute deity ended at the awful moment of that child's execution. Wiesel was probably saying that such a god as that must die—his existence makes no sense in the face of such horror. Yet there is another interpretation that Wiesel, as an artist, makes possible: God is known and exists in relationship to human suffering. He exists as a God who dies with us. We know God because we suffer, because we are horrified by injustice and senseless pain. We know God as a sufferer with us—He is there on the gallows. God is not the Almighty Absolute; He is the absolute knowledge that there are no absolutes. He is God-with-us. François Mauriac, French novelist and essayist, who once listened to Elie Wiesel tell the story of the unfurling black smoke and swollen tongues of the death camps, asked himself

> What did I say to him? Did I speak of that other Israeli, his brother, who may have resembled him—the Crucified, whose Cross has conquered the world? Did I affirm that the stumbling block to his faith was the cornerstone of mine, and that the conformity between the Cross and the suffering of men was in my eyes the key to that impenetrable mystery whereon the faith of his childhood had perished?

A person who understands what Mauriac is saying, or what meaning comes to us from Elie Wiesel's inner voice, will not likely be a creature of violence. Or, if he finds himself an unconscious or vengeful participant in violent action, he will confess that he has succumbed to the Demon of the Absolute. By confessing, he will discover the faculty for avoiding violence in the future.

"You cannot pray to the Absolute," writes the Russian philosopher Nikolai Berdyaev. "No dramatic meeting with it is possible. We call that the Absolute which has no relation to an other and has no need of an other. The Absolute is not a being, is not personality."

There is no sign of life, no sense of existence in the Absolute. The God who is at the heart of religion and known by the persistent disciple is not the Absolute. He is a moving, changing reality. He exists for us and with us. When humans attempt to think of God as Absolute, they succumb to the Demon who reveals an absolute monarch, a dictator. It is this fictitious tyrant who leads us to do bad things in the name of religion.

The Absolute demands world order. He demands that the world be put together in a certain way. We become the servants of this absolute and hence act as spokespersons for certain ideals. The Demon charms us with what seem to be obvious and worthy goals and ideals. We become rationalist servants of a program, a project, a grand scheme. Revolutionaries and those who seek to order the world according to some noble design are slaves of the Demon of the Absolute. When the world order begins to take the shape that the rationalist dreamers prescribe for it, violence or slavery will result.

In *The Brothers Karamozov,* Ivan says he does not accept God, nor does he accept God's world. I understand him. I have said to myself, if there is a God, then there should be order and harmony. There should be no unmerited suffering. Yet I look at myself, my behavior. I look at those I love. I see the horrors of world hunger and hear the frightening tales of possible nuclear destruction. I do not accept God, nor do I accept God's world. But think. What have I done? My reason has fashioned a God and a notion of world order. My reason has done this because it cannot stand its feeling of helplessness. It refuses to acknowledge that it is not in control, so it has created a delusion. Delusion ends in one of two ways: either it takes over the whole field of reality for us or it can be exposed for what it is. In this latter case, if I can expose God for not being the kind of Absolute I required in my delusion, I can then dispense with him and his phony world order. *I* am then left to do as I please.

Both ways of dealing with the delusion of the Absolute may lead to violence. If the delusion takes over the field of reality, I will become a fanatic and do whatever is necessary to contend against those who oppose my delusion. If I expose the delusion, I am free to be my own law and justify any action I wish.

In early-seventeenth-century Japan there were two feudal lords, Hideyori Toyotomi and Ieyasu Tokugawa, who sought to consolidate and unify Japan. They wanted to use the benefits of European trade to establish their positions as rulers. In order to do this they affirmed the need for beliefs that supported their own absolute power. The world order represented in the old feudal structure of their society was essential to their purposes. That world order was based on certain religious assumptions. The absolute power they sought for themselves required the support of an absolute religious world order. The result was an edict of persecution passed on 27 January 1614, designed to purge Japan of those religious leaders and systems that opposed their own absolute purposes.

The Demon of the Absolute likes a tidy world. It does not like us to live a balanced, moderate life. It does not like what it calls contradictions and paradoxes. In politics, for example, the Demon says to some of us,

"There must be no one who is recognized for having more wisdom, more knowledge or understanding than any other. The absolute power must be given to all the people. We must have a pure democracy where everyone has equal say in everything."

But then the Demon will say to someone else, "Look. The people are not wise enough to take care of themselves. They have no power, no wealth. Let us take care of them. We shall wield absolute power on their behalf."

The Demon does not want us to recognize that no power should be absolute, no power should go unchecked—not even the power of all the people. The secret of existence is balance and moderation, not absolutes. The Demon rejects the secret.

In religion the Demon says to some of us, "How can there be truth unless it is one thing and not another, not many things? Either God must be absolute and omnipotent or there is no God at all."

The Demon is not willing to acknowledge that it is possible to know truth without calling into question the possibility that someone else may know it differently. He will not accept that God is the one who calls all absolutes into question, that He does it by being with-us as we observe the world around us. The demon says to some believers, "Well, it is obvious that God is not personal. What? Can he be a big person some-where off in space? That is impossible. However, I am willing to admit that there is some kind of force, energy, that is greater than we are. It is an impersonal reality, though."

The Demon will not recognize that so long as it is a human being who observes that all of reality is more than it seems to be, it must also be true that what is observed is personal. The Demon does not like Heisenberg.

The Demon sometimes remarks, "The truth must be embodied in and preserved by an infallible church." To others he says, "No! The truth is something I will affirm for myself as an individual. I need no other authority, no church, no priest."

But the truth is not in either of these absolutes. Instead it lies in both claims and in the many variations that lie between them. However, it is not very likely that we shall know this truth and be able to resist the Demon unless we are disciples who descend like miners into the depths of religious traditions where the gold and the diamonds are stored. There we shall be freed from rationalistic scheming and be able to use our minds, enlightened and transformed. We shall be free of the Demon of the Absolute and be able to avoid further temptation to do bad things in the name of religion. I wonder, does he still sit there on my shoulder? Every time I turn around, he disappears. I must try to catch him unawares.

Ideas, Dreams, and Destiny

Ivan Morris has written a delightful account of tragic heroes in the history of Japan. Entitled *The Nobility of Failure*, it tells the stories of those individuals who faced defeat in the irrevocable collapse of causes they had championed. These heroes belong to the centuries of Japanese history from the fourth to the twentieth. The stories demonstrate the sincerity, bravery, and dignity of what is often in the eyes of the world thought of as defeat.

I was particularly taken with the tale of Yorozu, a very ordinary warrior of the sixth century who fought on the side of those forces loyal to the ancient traditions of Japan as represented by the imperial family. Yet Yorozu's battle was against very prominent members of that family who championed the corrupting innovations of Buddhism. The troops of the high officials were superior, but many brave and successful engagements were won by those on the losing side. Yorozu tries to escape, but returns to face insurmountable odds. He tricks his enemies, killing many of them, then cuts his bow in three pieces, bends his sword, and throws it into the river. Finally he seizes his dagger and stabs himself in the throat. "The Emperor's Shield," he called out, "that's what I wished to be, devoted to defending His Majesty. But no one knows who fights for what."

The point is that Yorozu did what he had to do. He did it well and honestly. That's what mattered, not the righteousness of the cause itself. It seems there may be moments in our existence when we discover that the whole business of living is a dilemma: we have chosen the path we will take and we have to accept the consequences. It is beneath human dignity to change paths or to be taken captive in order to survive. We learn that the only worthy aspect of living is wrapped up in the integrity of a decision, the courage to follow through. Yorozu learned that both forces fought for the same reason. They were both loyal to the emperor. The manner of their reasoning was different. Everything was uncertain, except the bravery of defeat.

Many of these stories simply accept the violence. There are causes that need defending. Defending a cause, or being loyal, are virtues in and of themselves. To question the cause is to discover that there is no occasion for doing the most important thing in life—being courageous, even in the circumstances of defeat.

Now, I don't know whether I could be as brave as Yorozu. Could I die for my country, right or wrong? Could I die for the corporation? Many people do, of course. They permit the stress of the company policy to damage their hearts, their digestive tracts. They devote themselves to the struggle for more money than they need, but as much as the executives suggest is possible. And they die for a lost cause. But somehow, I don't think that's the same as Yorozu's commitment. Yorozu sought no gain other than the imperial favor.

We might think that a person who lives only for such abstract virtues as courage and honesty has nothing else to live for. And perhaps that's true for some. Yorozu had a family he loved. They had to be put to death because the court decided Yorozu was a treacherous person. Perhaps there was nothing left for Yorozu. But what was left was the code—the code of selfless devotion.

It seems a bit like Martin Luther's discovery that sin is present in the noblest of our intentions and actions. His teaching of justification by grace through faith really ends up enabling us to say: "This is what I must do. It may not be right; but it's the best I can do, the *only* thing I can do in the circumstances."

There's a certain kind of liberation to that discovery. When I think about terrorists and revolutionaries, I think of Yorozu and Luther. Life does not usually present us with the possibility of being absolutely *right* about things. Life goes on, and seldom because it depended upon being right. Sometimes there are Holocausts, Hiroshimas. But life goes on. Of course, there are times when the right seems clearer than at other times—as in the case of the deliberate slaughter of millions of Jews by the Nazi high command. But mostly we have to recognize that we do the best we can—"God help me, I can do no other."

I find it difficult to condone violence, even for a seemingly just cause, because I know that the justice of all causes is tainted with inordinate self-interest and distorted to serve all kinds of motivations—often in service to the Demon of the Absolute. But I also know that often the terrorist or the revolutionary has nothing to live for but the courage to follow through on his commitment. He may become a hero, known only for the nobility of his defeat and failure. But perhaps he can do no other; he lives by the code of selfless devotion.

I think this notion is very important to anyone who wishes to understand violence, especially violence done in "the name of religion." Although it is true that I may do what is otherwise a bad thing, when I steal or destroy in order to get food for me and my family, I am much more likely to engage in violence either because I *recognize no code* of right or wrong except my desire or survival, or because I *serve a code*. As in the case of Yorozu, the code may be all I have. Now, in this book, we are interested in understanding violence done in the name of religion. So we ignore here the kind of violence done by those who maim and destroy without concern, reason, or code.

The Authority of Ideas

Violence done in service to a code is violence provoked and justified by an idea. Many of us have forgotten how significant ideas are. In the academic world we tend to emphasize environment and social setting in our attempts to interpret human behavior. The bad apple in the barrel is the product of a polluted barrel. But ideas have always generated action. They convey a certain authority—become the author of meaning. Ideas are carried by words; they are the way we think and communicate the assumptions that are at work in us. No one lives, thinks, or acts without assumptions. Assumptions are what make us unique as persons. And ideas are the way we work through what our assumptions are. Ideas are generated in relation to a social setting, to environmental circumstances, but they are not explained by it.

The fish has an idea of what it is to move about, to get from here to there—either for a purpose or just in order to move about. But the tortoise tells his friend the fish that he has just returned from a *walk* on the land. "Walk? What do you mean?" asks the fish, "I suppose you're talking about swimming." The tortoise has to explain that land is something firm, hard. You can't swim on land, he tells the fish; you have to walk. But, of course, the fish insists that land has to be like the sea, and that to move about it will be necessary to dive and swim. If the fish is ever to know what it is like to move about on land, he has to learn to see his idea of moving about in a different context. Otherwise he will never be able to converse with the tortoise about moving around. His idea is very important, but so likewise is the setting for it.

Yet I think we tend to downplay the significance of ideas today. We are so enamored of therapy and adjustment that we want to "fit in." In the academic world scholars are anxious to have everyone conform to the conventions of "the field," and they stress social factors in many of their attempts at explaining and interpreting. But sometimes an idea captures my mind and my imagination. I give myself to the idea because it is exciting. It's so right. And it's something I can give myself to. It becomes a dream—a goal, an end. Something worth fighting for. In a life where everything is uncertain, where existence is "just one damned thing after another," I may decide that it's time to abide by the courage of devotion to my idea, my dream. What else is there? Nothing but frustration in a world where nobody listens to my cry for meaning, my hope to be somebody, or my desire for some one thing that is holy and worthwhile.

Ideas and Passion

The conspirators responsible for the assassination of Egyptian president Anwar Sadat in October 1981 left a statement called "The Forgotten Duty."

> Is it not high time for those who have believed to humble their hearts to the Reminder of God and to the truth which He hath sent down; and that they should not be like those to whom the Book was formerly given and for whom the time was long, so that their hearts became hard, and many of them are reprobates?

It is easy for me to ask how anyone can be so fanatic. But I am not thinking about life very much if I cannot understand the devotion behind this constitution of terrorism. You see, many of us need to wake up to the fact that existence on our planet is in turmoil for want of ideas, for want of something to be passionate about other than the condition of our loins. We are so much captive to business as usual, so accustomed to accepting the stress and dehumanization of work, taxes, and litigation, that we ignore the passion in us. We reject the believer in us. And, of course, one way of rejecting the believer is to assume that all believers are terrorists who do bad things in the name of religion. Yet the record is clear, violence is also *rejected* by believers, good things are done by believers.

Opposition to the path of terrorism does not require us to deny the passionate ways of pilgrimage or poetry. It is necessary for human beings to walk in beauty. That requires insight, wisdom, dedication to ideas. It is a risk. But if humans take no risks, they possess no dignity, no honor. Some things may indeed be worth dying for. Dying with dignity may be an idea worth affirming.

There is some indication that we may be aware of our hunger for courage and belief. One of the heroes of our popular culture is a terrorist. Rambo is a weapons-trained survivalist. Recently an escapee from the Arizona prisons system survived for almost two months in the wilderness areas of the northern part of the state. The journalists began calling Danny Ray Horning "Rambo" because of the manner in which he was able to elude sheriff's deputies, state police, and bloodhounds. He kidnapped people at the point of a .44 magnum revolver, but didn't harm them. The media converted a dangerous convict into a hero. They called him "Rambo." "I don't know what they'll call me now," said Danny Ray after he was captured, "but I hope it's not Rambo. I'm not that way at all." He said he took hostages because he had to. When he traded shots with the state police during a chase, he said, "I came close to blowing the top of his head off." But when he threatened two women with his revolver he mused, "I wasn't going to hurt them. . . . I was realistic. I thought we'd get stopped and it would be time to give up."

Danny Ray Horning is no hero. But the media had many people fascinated with the romance of his cunning, his calculated courage, and his ability to survive. Horning is no Rambo, by his own admission, but he reminds us that there are values in life other than lawful behavior or just causes. Rambo reminds us of the same thing, but his courage is linked to survival at all costs and to his devotion to American ideals. He is a bit like Yorozu, except that his nobility is ascribed to his survival, not to his failure.

Those who are terrorists, or otherwise involved in violence that is linked with religious identity, are human beings. They are people who perceive that a whole way of life is threatened with extinction; or they are dedicated to ideas that are part of a last resolve. "This idea and the courage to die for it is all we have left."

What idea? American democracy? Christian civilization? Islamic truth? Scientific "objectivity"? Irish Protestant orthodoxy?

Ideas and Ideology

Professor Bruce Lawrence, in a study of what he calls "fundamentalism" among Jews, Christians, and Muslims, demonstrates that these *Defenders of God* are uncompromising supporters of ideologies, not of theologies. That is a very important distinction to make. The word "ideology" implies a set of ideas that are generated by the Demon of the Absolute. Many of us do not like to live with risk and uncertainty. We don't make good Abrahams who go out, not knowing where we are to go. When we face circumstances that unsettle our perception of reality, we begin to grumble among ourselves: "What is happening to our world? Are there not some things that are abiding, steadfast? There must be some ideas no one can challenge or take away from us. Things we really believe."

So they take these ideas, often out of the religious tradition that has been the story of their lives, and they make them into a manifesto, an instrument of protest. An ideology is a manifesto of ideas to be defended against all odds. It has been our experience in the Western world that a favorite place to locate ideas that may become part of a manifesto is in a text that is considered "sacred." If a text is the fundamental source, the unchallenged authority, for truth about human destiny, then obviously it is a good place to go hunting for an ideology. Whether the text is Torah, Qu'ran, or Bible, it may be used in the same way—as a source of fundamental ideas, taken out of context to serve the Demon of the Absolute.

But, as Professor Lawrence reminds us, ideology is not theology. Ideology arises in order to defend. Theology is the rational analysis and description of a set of symbols that have the power to transform our very perception or reality. Theology talks about God and salvation, about dharma and enlightenment. Theology speaks of a way of perceiving *ordinary* reality that is different from our ordinary perception of it. Theology may be nonsense, or it may speak of matters the ordinary mind is incapable of understanding. Theology is not ideology, although many people have used it for ideological purposes. The world hungers for ideas, but the secular mindset recognizes no ideas other than its own. The secular mind is unaware of its own ideology.

The Ideology of Secularity

The academic, political, economic, and cultural elite often operate *as if* reality is composed entirely of the decisions they make and the ideas they control. They assume there is no more to reality than what we make of it. Secular means "world"; a secularist *believes* this world is sufficient unto itself. A secularist is a believer who is religious in her own way. A secularist is a believer who thinks she is a nonbeliever. A secularist is quite sectarian about her beliefs. She does not permit much deviation. She does not realize that we always live not so much in a world as in a *perception* of the world. If a secularist is a believer in "this world," she must learn that the notion of "this world" is itself the result of a certain perception, a point of view, a belief that lives in a story about what is good and what is true.

The functions of business and politics and education are largely in the hands of secularists, believers in a "this-world" image of technical achievement and economic consumption. Among intellectuals and scholars, the "this-world" believers have assumed for a long time that any religious ideas other than their own are ignorant, superstitious, or merely anachronisms. They suppress "outsiders" either by ignoring them or by ridicule. They force "outsiders" to write only for their own "dishonored" journals and they keep them out of the academy by exiling them to "outsider" colleges and institutes. There is a covert violence at work that rejects honest dialogue and destroys careers and sometimes lives—all in the name of secularism, which is certainly an ideology if not a religion.

Resurgence of Traditional Religion

Today we observe religious resurgence all over the globe. By religious resurgence I mean renewed interest in traditional religion. That is to say, I'm not referring to my idea that religiousness is a universal human characteristic that finds expression in ways that may not be thought of as "religion." There is considerable evidence that the growth of so-called "fundamentalism" in the Islamic and Christian worlds is not a set of isolated statistics. In the United States, the so-called "mainline" churches (for example, Presbyterian, United Methodist, United Church of Christ, Episcopal) may not be growing, but that may be because they are too much identified with the established values of the liberal and secular order. The mainline probably does not represent an alternative experience, and religious resurgence usually represents a protest against religious stagnation. But membership is up among evangelicals and pentecostals (such as the Assemblies of God); and in countries like Brazil these groups are *overtaking* the resurgence of interest in African-Latino sects and cults.

There is also a growing interest in Native American wisdom. The popularity of fiction like that of Tony Hillerman is evidence not only of the search for entertaining stories and detective thrillers, but also a quest for mystery and for alternative views of reality. The New Age phenomenon is difficult to assess, but it is prodigious, as evidenced by the sale of books describing the hidden knowledge and energy of the universe and of secret societies.

In the spring of 1991 I spent a semester in a lovely American city, Tulsa, Oklahoma. I served as a distinguished visiting professor at the University of Tulsa. Fifteenth Street in Tulsa is a charming array of cafes, good restaurants, antique shops, and the Cherry Street Bakery, which, incidentally, has the best sourdough bread I have yet discovered. But there is also the "Peace of Mind Bookstore," which I visited time and again. It was a fascinating place, with very interesting people and fabulous books that, like works of art, exist to create a reality unlike what I must ordinarily live.

Natsume Sōseki (Kinosuki), a Japanese writer of the early twentieth century, captures my mood about art and religion. "I want a poem," he wrote in his novel *The Three-Cornered World*, "which abandons the commonplace, and lifts me, at least for a short time, above the dust and grime of the workaday world. . . . The trademark of the majority of [contemporary] playwrights and novelists is their inability to take even one step out of this world."

The point is, there is no proper way to perceive this world without being able to step out of it. I stepped out of it when I entered the "Peace of Mind Bookstore." All of my academic cynicism directed against these "weird" people with their curious books and pendants—all of it left me. I visited the store many times and discovered a highly intellectual and imaginative clientele. I have since discovered those same bookstore communities in my own city and know that they exist all across the country—strangely enough especially in the vicinity of universities, those bastions of secularist orthodoxy.

What does this resurgence mean? For our purposes in this book it means a rebellion against the secular assumptions about reality is taking place. The people accept whatever *good* the orders of business and technology will produce, but the people are not concerned with the kind of "consistency" the secularist mind requires. By intuition they know there is more to reality than the scientific and intellectual priesthood dictates. The people are interested in ideas that help to transcend the routinality of existence. They are interested in ways of perceiving the "whole" of things, and of transforming their lives into a meaningful path of destiny.

The people turn to evangelicalism, pentecostalism, New Age phenomena, Native American wisdom, because they are not afraid of their religiousness. They are aware of it and refuse to ignore it—as so often does the power elite of our society. The power elite, of course, ignore their religiousness at great risk. Nothing in human experience is so insidious as that which goes unrecognized. No "superstitions" are so devastating as the "superstitions" of the supposedly "irreligious." No violence in the name of religion is quite so insensible as that which is incapable of naming its own perceptions of ultimate order and meaning, or is unaware of its own story.

Impermanence and Impotence

Much of the violence done in the name of religion is an ideological response to change. Human beings, in their effort to discern some kind of order and meaning for existence, observe change and have to come up with some way of handling it. Some people are terrified by their observation of change. The greater and more rapid the experience of change, the greater their terror becomes. Change is the one constant of human experience, but in our past history we have often been able to deal with it because it has not been devastating or immediately threatening. In what we call the "modern" world, change is kaleidoscopic and chaotic, except for those who are directly involved as instruments of change. When change invites terror among those who have no role in the process, it produces terrorists, those who create terror by acting out their own terror.

Change is the one constant of human experience, but we create myths of stability and changelessness when faced with changes in which we have no controlling share. At the time of the Reformation of the sixteenth century in Europe, there were those who were helpless in the face of a changing society. They began to imagine a time of original order and stability that they could have a hand in restoring. They thought of it as "New Testament times" or the time before the Roman Emperors Constantine and Theodosius "changed" Christianity to suit their political needs. But there has never been a time without change; without change there would be no time. There is no consistency to history, no pattern of change and stability. There is only one thing and another—only change.

Ah, but yes, we have an *idea* of stability and changelessness. And wherever it comes from, it is important because it enables us to live with change without becoming a plaything on the wind. It enables us to be *participants* in change.

To be a plaything on the wind is terrifying for many of us. Many scientists and technologists live with change because they are its agents. But change is something that involves not just capitalistic entrepreneurs, investors, and engineers. Change is not something to be imposed upon the rest of us by a power elite. Nor is it only a matter of one group of humans forcing change upon another. It involves *all* of being, not just some "important" humans, not even just all humans, but animals and rivers, seas and skies, stars and moons. To be able to understand this is to be the exemplar of a profoundly religious sensibility that will avoid doing violence. But many agents of change are instruments of violence because their changes do not concern themselves with the participation of all "others"—all of being—in their agenda of change.

When northern Europeans came to colonize the North American continent in the seventeenth century, they imposed many kinds of change upon the Native Americans and their environment. They brought disease and disrupted the social order of the natives and their relationship to each other and the land. The Europeans spoke of the Devil and of spells and witchcraft. They accused the natives of practicing evil rituals. But when the natives experienced epidemics and great tensions among their people, they began to accept the fear of witches and sometimes responded as violent mobs.

In the late seventeenth century Matthew Mayhew told the story of George, a native who suffered from impotence and torment, and turned for help to a well-known shaman. By this time many of the natives had adopted the idea that suffering and misfortune were the work of spirits who were conjured up by people with evil intention and power. The shaman diagnosed George's troubles as witchcraft and began an exorcism ritual in which he danced around a fire while George and other sick people lay around the circle. However, the Indians claimed the shaman himself had bewitched the sick. They broke up the dance and threatened to burn him unless he cured the sick man. Change invites violence whenever the ordinary ways of managing misfortune do not work or satisfy.

After all, a certain amount of misfortune and suffering is a constant element in the flow of change, isn't it? I mean, hardly a day goes by that I am not a bit upset by some threat to the assumed order of my life. I get a bill for which I hadn't budgeted. The company neglects the raise in salary on which I counted. My neighbor threatens me with a lawsuit. My taxes are too high. I don't like a computer age, but I have no choice but to adapt. I face unwanted surgery. All of these circumstances are distressing and I get angry—sometimes I don't know at what. I just get angry. I may hit the wall. I may throw darts at a cutout of the president. I may race my Chevy through a residential zone. There may be a brief moment of cursing and foul language. Or, I may take a bantam rooster and make it fight for me. I may take a lamb and bloody its life on an altar where I offer it up to whatever powers that be, as the flesh of the best and worst in me. I may go to mass where I confess that I am a sinner and receive the "Body and Blood of Christ" who takes my anger into his death and offers me new and uninterrupted life.

We must have some way of expressing the anger and torment in us. There must be a way to take care of violence. And it has to be more than just going to a counselor who asks me, "How do you feel about that?" The violence I feel deep inside me hasn't only to do with getting along with friends, neighbors, and lovers. It has to do with having a place in the total scheme of things. Violence is cosmological, not psychological. It has to do with knowing what to do about relentless change and my identity in the midst of change. Who am I and what am I in all this?

Is There a Destiny That Shapes Us?

The experience of change leads to a preoccupation with destiny. America is a nation of people who live with a special story about destiny. Destiny always shaped our self-understanding—at least until well past the middle of the twentieth century of our way of reckoning change. In our public addresses, our music, our art we have celebrated a sense of becoming, of going somewhere, of having a purpose to our existence. Change is not just one damned thing after another for Americans. We are going somewhere. Things add up. We are on a mission, a pilgrimage. From the days of the Puritans of Plymouth and Massachusetts Bay we have been a people "in covenant with God," a "city upon a hill," or Abraham Lincoln's "last, best hope of earth."

This sense of destiny, the idea of direction connected with change, has been important to our need for identity. Who am I? I am American.

To be human is to be American. Is there any other way for me to be human? Outsiders to this covenant people need our help, our goodness, our example. They, too, may some day be invited into the covenant. Destiny always has to do with salvation. After all, what is salvation but being salved—healed, made whole, put back together.

When some Christians talk of being concerned with salvation, they may have in mind "going to heaven." Why are the people so interested in "heaven" as a state to be in or a "place" to go when we die? Why, simply because they know that much of their lives makes no sense whatsoever if this is all there is. Ordinary existence is chaotic, disappointing, disjointed. It needs mending, healing. It needs to be part of a whole that gives it purpose and hope. It needs salving, saving—salvation as a promise of meaning beyond "this veil of tears."

Well now, some of us may not be so concerned about salvation as "going to heaven." But we still look for assurance that there is *more*, that there is purpose. We want to be part of a whole. We, too, want salvation, and that means we are concerned with destiny. The American story has been a story of salvation and destiny. Our language, our music, and our art and literature, are filled with religious images of salvation and destiny.

The Violence of *Manifest* Destiny

If we remember that human beings always fall short of their own best intentions and ideals, we certainly understand that all good things can be used to violent ends. American destiny is a religious image that has sometimes been used to unjust and violent ends. The notion that we are a special people—the last, best hope of earth—has sometimes led us to impose our most selfish designs upon other people, other nations. The idea of "Manifest Destiny," for example, is a distortion of the basic symbol of a people in covenant. "Manifest Destiny," in the nineteenth century, had come to mean "We must save other peoples from their own folly; we must use the natural resources of the rest of the world to support our own sacred dreams of success."

We have engaged in violent actions—from the Spanish-American War to the War in Southeast Asia—in service to ideas of "Manifest Destiny." And, recently, as we participated in discussions with other nations in an "Earth Summit" in Rio de Janeiro, we reserved the "right" to do nothing in saving the earth that would jeopardize the American economy. We assume that only the United States has the right to our present standard of living, and we know that our present economic well-being depends upon violence to the earth and a kind of covert violence against the aspirations of other people. Our interpretations of our religious sense of destiny constantly express themselves in economic and political policies and maneuvers that inflict violence upon others. Violence in the name of religion!

Now, some of our intellectuals and academics assume that the violence done in the name of American destiny means the symbol itself is evil and must be suppressed. The idea of special destiny, they remind us, was used to maintain a social and political order that oppressed women, African Americans, and Native Americans. More violence done in the name of religion. The question is, however, how can we exist meaningfully in the midst of relentless change without an idea of destiny, without a symbol that reminds us we are part of a whole that is greater than the sum of its parts? Life does not and cannot depend entirely upon human choice and action. That would be a fate that renders us less than human. The point is, the Native American, the African-American, and the female presence among us are not innocent bystanders or righteous revolutionaries. They share the human condition. They inflict violence in the name of their own religious presuppositions about the order and meaning of existence. They, too, are constantly guilty of great "sins" of omission (many of which they are unaware) and commission.

It is possible to find meaning in the symbol of American destiny without deliberately inflicting violence. A city upon a hill is not necessarily a crusader's citadel, like the many abandoned fortresses I saw on a tour of Israel some years ago. A city upon a hill can be the sacred environs in which a people walk in beauty. What John Winthrop imagined, in his famous seventeenth-century address that gave the American story its image of the "city upon a hill," was a model of interdependent existence.

> We must entertain each other in . . . affection [he wrote], we must be willing to abridge ourselves of our superfluities for the supply of others' necessities. . . . We must delight in each other; make others' conditions our own; rejoice together, mourn together, labor and suffer together, always having before our eyes our commission and community in the work as members of the same body.

Of course, Winthrop's idea of the city upon a hill must be nurtured and taught. Otherwise it will succumb to self-serving notions like that of Manifest Destiny. There is something about the idea of the city upon a hill that always transcends the smaller interpretations we give it. As a matter of fact, it is a beautiful image, an image of beauty and harmony—a city upon a hill, all eyes upon it. It twinkles like a star in the night and gleams in the sunlight. Like a castle nestled among the trees along the Rhine, it invites mystery; it lifts the spirit and reminds us that ideas are dreams that are linked to our destiny in a changing cosmos.

The idea of destiny unites people, gives them a common sense of direction and purpose. If we lose our image of American destiny just because it has been used to violent ends, we lose the possibility of rediscovering our relationship to each other and to the earth we inhabit. Instead we will delight in those of the same color and education. We will never make the conditions of "others" our own; we will rejoice and mourn, labor and suffer only as robots programmed to do so in a system that reduces human existence to function and consumption. In the system that controls our existence today people must function *efficiently*—they must be resources. *Bodies* must function efficiently—they must be oiled, have their parts replaced; they must perform sexual acts upon request and do them well. Society will be replaced by system.

Society requires freedom and ideas; it requires dreams and visions of destiny. Society is an organism of free individuals, bound by a common destiny. Society requires a creative exercise of human religiousness, which is a bold commitment to the fact that we are always more than we *know*, more than we think we are, more than the measure we take of ourselves and others. Regardless of where we sit in the scheme of things, there is a destiny that shapes our ends.

We can see evidence of this among our literary artists. The artist is always a rebel. She is possessed by a religious spirit that tells her that life is more than what most of us settle for. She is aware of the need to walk meaningfully, to do it in beauty. This is why Annie Dillard can take us with her on a pilgrimage among all the bugs and bushes, the muskrats and the mock orange, of *Tinker Creek* where she can write of all the sparks of soul that emerge and cling to us. She can show us that what we *usually* say of such things as God and religion are mere tranquilizers of an establishment, merely ways to settle for a life without risk, without dream or destiny. "Each thing in the world is translucent," she writes in a little book called *Holy the Firm*, "even the cattle, and moving, cell by cell. I remember this reality. Where has it been? I sail to the crest of the hill as if blown up the slope of a swell. I see, blasted, the bay transfigured below me, the saltwater bay, far down the hill past the road to my house, past the firs and the church and the sheep in the pasture: the bay and the islands on fire and boundless beyond it, catching alight the unraveling sky." At another point, after showing us how everything is of a piece, but distinguishable, she tells us:

> These are only ideas, by the single handful. Lines, lines, and their infinite points! Hold hands and crack the whip, and yank the Absolute out of there and into the light, God pale and astounded, spraying a spiral of salts and earths, God footloose and flung. And cry down the line to his passing white ear, "Old Sir! Do you hold space from buckling by a finger in its hole? O Old! Where is your other hand?" His right hand is clenching, calm, round the exploding left hand of Holy the Firm.

Why do Annie Dillard, Edward Abbey, Wendell Berry, Peter Mathiessen, Barry Lopez—and Loren Eiseley before them—reach out into the world of science and deeply into those realms of experience we call "nature"? Is it not because they are asserting their liberation from the standard ways of perceiving the relentless march of change? They are searching for what we have always known as our destiny. They have discovered freedom in the ideas created by images, symbols. They have discerned a new relationship with everything around them and they express it in words that set things in ultimate order and meaning. These are not people of violence; their religion is like the Second Coming of Christ. Yet, like Christ, they may do some violence!

Abbey wrote of the "monkey-wrench gang," who would do things to slow up the mindless juggernaut of bureaucrats, developers, and financiers. He advocated throwing "monkey wrenches" into the jaws of "progress." He created some violence in the name of his religion, just as did the Nazarene when he said, "Get the hell out of the temple unless you want to tend to the sacred rites of the temple!"

We live in a world where violence is always taking place. I suffer violence at the hands of those who believe that the manipulation of money is a sacred law, notarized by God. They do violence when they determine at their pleasure what I must pay to live, how I must pay it, and, indeed, *how* I shall live. Perhaps the time has come when I must do some bad things to protest the violence that offends me when it creates dehumanized people without homes. After all, my religious perceptions do not condone that kind of violence; and, sooner or later, I must decide whether I can wait until the business world determines that it has sufficiently violated the temple of the earth and its personal conscience and that it's time to stop.

Perhaps I can't wait any longer. Perhaps my insight into the meaning of existence will tell me it is time to throw monkey wrenches or start kicking the money changers out of the temple. Like Yorozu, I may die in the process because I would be fighting against insurmountable odds. And David does not always slay Goliath. Perhaps I die only with the knowledge that I had to do what I had to do, that there is nobility in failure. Christ is always a failure. That's a law of existence. But he rises again! That's also a law of existence. The bodhisattva gives up her own ultimate enlightenment in order to suffer compassionately for all sentient beings.

The Way
of the Pilgrim

We have thought together about many issues. That has been my goal—to show the complexity and depth of the concern for violence done in the name of religion. Religions exist in order to help us understand and contend with the violence in us, whether done in the name of religion or not. It is *people* who do violence, not religions. Religions are used by all of us as a way of finding identity, as a means of telling us who we are and how we shall behave. But *all* of us are religious—at least we have been throughout history. Whether we identify ourselves with religion or not, we are religious; and our religiousness expresses itself in our art, our politics, our music, our economics. As religious beings we may do violence in the name of a theory, a cause, or a nation that assumes the same role as religions do. It does no good to blame violence on religion just because some who are identified by religion make use of it to sanctify violence. Perhaps we are the champions of a cause or a theory that we defend self-righteously in a distinctively religious manner.

Religions are not only a means of human identification, but also repositories of a wisdom that is not ordinarily understood except by those who ask questions and are willing to be taught as disciples. In all of our experience, including religion, there is the temptation of the Demon of the Absolute who may easily incite us to defend his honor. And sometimes there is not much we can do, other than what we *have* to do—even if it entails some form of violence. There is power in ideas, in dreams of a better world. There is the need to find direction in the midst of relentless change. And there are frustration and failure. These are all factors that may involve us in violence. There seems to be little chance of escaping the doing of violence, either overt or covert. But there is a way to understand it and to improve and dignify the human journey in spite of it. That way is the way of the pilgrim.

Even as I write these chapters I hear of many things that go on in the world, many of them seeming to be connected in some way with religion. I read a small headline in the newspaper: "No end in sight to N. Irish fight, both sides say." The article told of the killing of a Roman Catholic policeman in front of his wife and three children as they arrived for mass at St. Gabriel's Retreat, a monastery seventy miles southeast of Belfast. Every time I read of such terrors in Ireland, in Lebanon, in India—anywhere in the world—I want to cry out: "How long? How long will it go on? Is there no end? How does a person come to the conclusion that his 'cause' gives him the right to bomb, to shoot, to stab innocent people? Who are you to do this? What kind of a person are you? Do you have no conscience? Do you really believe you are justified?" Yet I feel, with Julian of Norwich, that "sin is behovely, but all shall be well, and all shall be well, and all manner of thing shall be well."

The evil goes on and on. I begin to wonder: Could we put a stop to such terrible actions if we began to regulate all behavior by chemical and medical means? Perhaps the solution to the great evils in this world is to be found in technology. If we can get to the point where we can govern ourselves by technical adjustments, then we will have no need for religion. As a child of the modern world, I have asked myself variations of that question many times.

Then I remember Aldous Huxley's story, *Brave New World.* It is a world that seems to have the capacity for regulating everything, even breeding people who will perform certain jobs, certain functions necessary to society, but who will be satisfied with their station in life. Everything is controlled. When one character gets depressed, he takes a dose of soma and all manner of things is well. But we begin to notice, in the story, that certain rituals are necessary to maintain a configuration of order and meaning, even in this technologically restrained world where all is "beyond freedom and dignity." There are also misfits in the "brave new world"—those who long for a sense of the past, of history, those who would rather have freedom than security or painlessness.

I believe the sacrifice of our freedom, our transcendence of biological necessity, is too great a price to pay for ridding the world of pain and sorrow. It is too great a price for the technological temples in which humanity will reside in the future. I, too, would be a misfit in such a world and I shall be happy to have left the world before it is totally brave and new. Yet I am already a misfit. A misfit is a pilgrim who moves slowly and carefully through this world with no ultimate commitment to its latest wiles.

The pilgrim deplores the bad things that are done in the name of religion, but he does not often give way to the violence within himself, and he knows that it is more human to have the freedom to do good or evil than it is to have evil controlled at the expense of our humanity. He understands his own inclinations to evil and is not quick to judge others. He knows how to live with the tension between the fact that religions exist because people do bad things and the need to believe in a future well-being.

The Japanese novelist Shusako Endo has published several stories that deal with the unique ways people of different cultures receive the truths of the same religion. Endo's own life has been a pilgrimage, a search to discover what his Catholic baptism means in the midst of a pragmatic Japanese world where the idea of a transcendent God is difficult to comprehend. His fiction portrays that pilgrimage in many different modes. There is violence in these stories; they tell us what happens when one perception of the world encounters another.

The Wonderful Fool is the account of a misfit, a rather simple foreigner, the Frenchman Gaston Bonaparte, who makes his way into Japan through the life of a typical Japanese family. Gaston is an awkward, bungling figure. He has the face of a horse, is slovenly in dress and boorish in manner. He apparently lacks common sense and cringes before any hint of danger. Yet he hurls himself into one menacing situation after another. People are repulsed by Gaston or seek to take advantage of him; but they are confronted by a self-sacrificing love that makes them uncomfortable and forces them to face up to themselves. We see change take place in even the most ruthless of persons. The selfish young career girl Tomoe, who has no time for sentiment or anything else except her own gain, finally says of Gaston:

> A man with a simple love for others, trusting everyone; who no matter how often he is deceived or betrayed, continues to keep his flame of love and trust from going out—such a man is bound to seem a fool in the world as it is today. But he is no ordinary fool. He is a wonderful fool.

We may have some difficulty with the simple character of Gaston. In some ways he is indeed a fool, a naive blunderer. He does not seem to take deliberate action. Instead he moves compulsively. Perhaps he is not to be taken as a model, but is instead an example of what happens when human society encounters those who do not live their lives according to its values.

Gaston does not keep things inside. He is not motivated by the need to succeed. Nor does he accept violence and unkindness stoically, cynically, or matter-of-factly. He cries and cowers and goes on trusting. He trusts others beyond their desire to be trusted. He is a pilgrim moving through a selfish, violent world. He represents an alien religiousness that initially arouses the violent reactions of people. His religiousness may have no label. His is a wandering presence that does not sanction a "brave new world" where efficiency and success are the values that justify behavior.

Endo's *The Samurai* is a novel about an encounter between Christians and traditional Japanese in the seventeenth century. Velasco is a Franciscan priest with very heroic notions of his role as a missionary to Japan. He is very ambitious and has a difficult time reconciling his selfish desires with the Christian faith. But in his own mind he succeeds. In his own mind Velasco believes God wants the Japanese people to know the passion of the Gospel and that he must be bishop of Japan. In the end he must confess that he has used the Japanese people to his own purposes; however, he continues to believe that his actions have been in accordance with God's will.

The envoys Velasco escorts on a voyage to Mexico and Spain are encouraged to convert to Christianity in order to impress Christian authorities with the interest of the Japanese in Christianity and in trade with New Spain. One envoy, the samurai Hasekura, has no honest intention of being a Christian. He is repulsed by the ugliness and pathos of the figure on the cross that he sees everywhere in Mexico and Europe. Spain and the Church decide against further trade with Japan. Even while Velasco and the envoys are on their diplomatic voyage, Japan has increased its persecution of Christians and closed its doors to the West.

Velasco returns to the Philippines to be superior of the Franciscan monastery. The envoys return to Japan, where they become scapegoats and pawns for the political maneuvering of the feudal lords. Hasekura is to be executed for becoming a Christian, accompanied to his death by the one who was "despised and rejected of men." Velasco, too, disobeys orders and returns to Japan where he is captured and burned at the stake.

In this novel we observe the manipulation and violence that occur as a result of the encounter of two world perceptions, two religions. As I read *The Samurai*, I began to realize something I had not understood before, at least not in the depth of my being. We like to reject those people and ideas that conflict with our own self-image, ambitions, and desires. In doing so, we reject our own ultimate good because goodness can only be found when the good of all is served. If I hold out for my own version of what is good for me, I will never discover goodness. Goodness suffers from my willfulness. But once I begin to realize this, goodness begins to triumph.

The person who learns this simple truth moves through life as a pilgrim. He thinks his own thoughts, but he is not attached to them, because he knows that goodness is more than he can know. He has his own convictions and commitments, but they are disciplines—rules for living. He is not attached to them because he understands that the truth that makes his life possible is greater than his commitments; his commitments have taught him this. The pilgrim is not a violent person, but he is religious, and he may have become wise through the discipline of his religion.

Velasco's martyrdom was the martyrdom of a European Christian. He served the cause of a glorified Christ who wished to share his compassion with a part of the world that could not comprehend his image. Velasco was a man of passion and ambition, a man with a sense of the heroic. He had to learn that his own dedication to the compassionate Christ must lose its impetuosity. It had to become less violent for true goodness to be served.

Hasekura too, was martyred, but he was not the same kind of Christian as Velasco. He had never taken the rituals of his native religion very seriously. The religious character of his culture had made him a person who would accept life with the tranquility and deep, placid smile of the Buddha. So Hasekura accepts his fate and discovers that the ugly man on the cross is his companion through the passion and suffering of death. Both men are pilgrims. They are the victims of the violence done by those who have identified their own ambitions, desires, and commitments as worthy of absolute loyalty.

When I think of what a pilgrim is, I do not think only of the black-suited adventurers of Plymouth Colony, standing with broad-brimmed hats and buckled shoes, muskets raised in apprehension of what the wilderness might bring forth. Still, those Massachusetts Puritans were pilgrims. They had left the security of one place to make their way in another. They were wayfarers, certainly, travelers on behalf of a way of life, a path.

Nor do I think only of hundreds of bedraggled wanderers making their way to Canterbury under the watchful eye of Geoffrey Chaucer. Pilgrimages to Lourdes, to Fatima, Chimaya, or Guadalupe; to Jerusalem, Benares, Mecca, Ise, or Kyoto—these are the travels of those who seek to touch the sacred. The true model for the way of the pilgrim may be Siddhartha Gautama or Jesus of Nazareth.

"In all the beauty of my early prime," says Gautama, "with a wealth of coal-black hair untouched by grey—despite the wishes of my parents, who wept and lamented—I cut off my hair and beard, donned a yellow robe and went forth from home to homelessness."

The pilgrim I have in mind is one who is aware of a kind of homelessness. He senses that he is *in* the world but not *of* it. "Foxes have holes, birds of the air have nests, but the Son of Man has nowhere to lay his head."

This may not mean that all pilgrims become wandering, homeless ascetics, but it does mean they discover and nurture this homelessness. To become too attached to place and property is to become one who will be forced into violence in order to acquire territory and defend it.

Loren Eiseley, twentieth-century naturalist and anthropologist, was a pilgrim. Speaking of Homer's *Odyssey*, he once wrote: "Odysseus's passage through the haunted waters of the eastern Mediterranean symbolizes, at the start of the Western intellectual tradition, the sufferings that the universe and his own nature impose upon homeward-yearning man."

Eiseley's writings are filled with this sense of the "homeward yearning." But it is an unsatisfied quest. Home is never found. Perhaps that is because it is necessary to discover that what we seek is not available in the ordinary course of things. After Gautama's enlightenment, he realized that "rebirth is no more; I have lived the highest life; my task is done; and now for me there is no more of what I have been."

The pilgrim simply realizes what is true for all of us: we are restless beings because we transcend the world in which we exist. "Our hearts are restless," said St. Augustine, "until they find their rest in thee."

The pilgrim disciplines his homelessness. He works at the Quest, the "homeward yearning," and tries to control his restlessness. Discipline and direction are the heart of religious tradition. Yet discipline and direction will not make sense to outsiders, to those who have not discovered their pilgrim status. Those who do not ask the right questions will never see the importance of pursuing answers.

T. S. Eliot gives us words to express this dilemma:

> When the Stranger says: "What is the meaning of this city?
> Do you huddle close together because you love each other?"
> What will you answer? "We all dwell together
> To make money from each other?" or "This is a community?"
> And the Stranger will depart and return to the desert.
> O my soul, be prepared for the coming of the stranger,
> Be prepared for him who knows how to ask questions.

The pilgrim is on quest, is himself the Stranger. He asks questions, then departs and returns to the desert. He understands homelessness and makes it a virtue. His homelessness makes it unlikely that there will be violence, bad things, done in the name of religion.

> By the grace of God I am a Christian man, by my actions a great sinner, and by calling a homeless wanderer of the humblest birth who roams from place to place. My worldly goods are a knapsack with some dried bread in it on my back, and in my breastpocket a Bible. And that is all.

These are the opening words of the anonymously published nineteenth-century Russian classic *The Way of a Pilgrim*. The author describes a life that is difficult for us to conceive. In virtually every way we can imagine, our lives are defined by what we can acquire and control. Life is an affair of getting information that we do not have in order that we may gain advantage over others. The advantage is in terms of power and wealth. It is virtually impossible for me to see the basic violence of this kind of world. For me it is all virtue; there have been so many "improvements" in life. I can only see the good of it all for me. The pilgrim seems a strange, ascetic figure of a bygone era, a pathetic character; he is obviously maladjusted, needs therapy to help him fit into the social grouping of our society.

"Pilgrimages," writes Harvey Cox, "instill the belief that people need not remain mired in any situation. They can 'move with God.' Pilgrimages are movements, but ruling groups want people either to remain quiescent—to stay where they are—or to go where they are sent."

Pilgrims are restless ones who are always on the move, never mired. Too many pilgrims would constitute a revolution. The world as we know it would be out of control and the comptrollers would be in serious trouble. I have described the pilgrim as a model for living in a violent world. Obviously, we shall not all leave home and family and move into box canyons, or take to the highways and byways. Nonetheless, we can all acknowledge that our restlessness is the result of our nature—we are more than we seem to be. We can confess the violence that is in us, that we share with the most reprehensible of terrorists. We can be prepared to move lightly and quickly, to deny the modern passion for power and property. We can discipline our homeward-yearning journey by learning to ask the questions that lie at the center of philosophic and religious traditions.

At the heart of the pilgrim's way is the knowledge that he is free. He is bound to no system. He has nothing to defend and lives only to care for everything that is—from the meanest beast to the most repulsive assassin. His only loyalty is to those who are in need and to the discipline that has taught him the art of caring. One of the spiritual disciplines in *The Way of the Pilgrim* is the prayer-without-ceasing, the "Jesus prayer" as it is frequently called. The person who adopts this discipline finds the prayer welling up within him, in his breathing, the beat of his heart, often when he least expects it.

In the book, the pilgrim tells us that he was taken by some children into the beautiful garden of a large country house. He was very warmly received into a household that delighted in visits with passing pilgrims. "While I was speaking," he says, "a strong feeling came over me, urging me to withdraw within myself again. . . . I therefore got up, saying, 'Please excuse me, but I must leave now. . . . ' But the hostess replied: 'Oh, no! God forbid that you should go away. I won't allow it. My husband, who is a magistrate, will be coming back from town this evening, and how delighted he will be to see you!'"

The pilgrim is free to be where he is needed, but he cannot always control his coming and going. That is because none of us knows where he is really needed and for how long. The pilgrim must be free even of his desire to meditate, to pray, or to nurture his solitude and freedom. He must be free to exist for others. His journey is never finished, but there are stops that must be made.

The sacred shrines and temples of many of the world's religions remind us of this. Kosuke Koyama tells of visiting the famous Shwe Dagon Pogoda on Singuttara Hill in Rangoon, Burma. The height of the Pagoda is 344 feet and its perimeter at the base is 1,476 feet. The visitor must remove shoes and socks and trudge up the long hill under the hot sun. As a result, when he arrives at the foot of the Pagoda, his mind is prepared for the visit. Many such shrines have extended approaches, sometimes as long as a mile or more. No bicycles or motor vehicles are permitted. Everyone must walk. "The holy must be approached slowly and carefully with respect and humility." The shrine builders may have been violent persons, sometimes constructing their holy places with the sweat and the tears of the poor, often concerned only with making their temples superior to those of another sect. Yet the tradition they represented understood the slow and humble way of the pilgrim.

The world in which we live does not like the pilgrim, of course. It will not leave him or his conscience alone. It reminds him that even though he is not a doer of violence himself, he is guilty of violence that he does not directly or consciously condone. Here we encounter the heart of the problem. Many bad things may be done in the name of religion even though the pilgrim is not a violent person. Gautama does not do bad things in the name of religion (he is a pilgrim), but some Buddhists do. Jesus does not do bad things in the name of religion, but some Christians do.

I may say, "Well, what has that to do with me? I keep myself free and purified of violence." If I take this position, you should immediately begin to recognize a certain phoniness, even callousness, in my claim. If I begin to explore the heart of my tradition's teachings, I will probably discover that the pilgrim always understands not only that he is never completely purified of violence and thoughts of it, but that he is somehow involved in violence that he does not intend. He is responsible for the violence of others. The violence of others also requires him to serve those who suffer from the violence. That is why, in the Mahayana traditions of Buddhism, the person who becomes enlightened also knows that he must live with those who have not attained Buddha-nature. Therefore, he must be willing to suffer with them, to live in compassion with all sentient beings. In some sense, his own enlightenment is incomplete without the enlightenment of all. The way of the pilgrim is never an escape into isolated purity or irresponsibility.

Christianity in the modern world has nurtured a kind of salvationism that is concerned primarily with the claims of its own holiness and the pleasant security of being "born again." This salvationism was expressed long ago in the writings of John Wesley:

A Methodist is one who has the love of God shed abroad in his heart.
. . . His heart is full of love to all mankind and is purified from envy,

wrath, malice, and every unkind affection. . . . He keeps all God's com-
mandments . . . follows not the customs of the world. . . . He cannot
speak evil of his neighbour any more than he can lie. . . . He does good
unto all [persons]. . . . These are the principles *and practices* of our
communion. These are the marks of a true Methodist. By these alone
do Methodists desire to be distinguished from all other [persons]. (italics
added)

I do not judge John Wesley. He said many things in many different
contexts. Here he tries to justify the Methodist movement in the eyes of
those who disapprove. Still, we may wonder how many Methodists there
are, or ever have been, according to this measure. We may also wonder
whether such claims are the mark of a true pilgrim. Instead, a Catholic
Christian might well recall that the heart of Christian ritual life is a
recitation again and again of words such as:

We confess that we have sinned against thee *in thought, word, and
deed, by what we have done, and by what we have left undone. We* have
not loved thee with our whole heart; *we* have not loved our neighbors
as ourselves. *We* are truly sorry and *we* humbly repent. (italics mine)

That is why the pilgrim begins his book: "By the grace of God I am a
Christian man, by my actions a sinner." The pilgrim knows that life is a
matter of "we" not "I"; it is a pilgrimage with neighbors, seen and
unseen. What is undone is as much with us as what is done. What is
done by others claims our attention as much as our own actions.

Among the desert fathers it was said that Abba Macarius had gone
one day to the marsh to find some leaves for drying and weaving. On his
return he met the devil on the road. The Evil One struck him repeatedly
with a scythe that he carried. But Abba Macarius paid him no attention.
"Ah, Macarius," said the devil, "I have done everything you do. You fast,
so do I; you keep vigil, I do not sleep at all. So why am I powerless
against you? I think I know. There is but one thing you do that beats
me." Abba Macarius asked what that was. "Your humility," replied the
devil. "Because of that I have no power against you." Humility is present
in the pilgrim because he knows that since human responsibility is a
matter of "we" not "I," he can only go through life as a confessing and
compassionate one.

Beginning more than a half-century ago, the American theologian
Reinhold Niebuhr sought to remind us that justice in this life is more
than a matter of good personal intentions or private morality. An individual, said Niebuhr, may be quite capable of considering interests other

than his own. He may seek to do good. He may be able to do this as a person arriving at some rational decision or acting on some ultimate commitment. He may, therefore, avoid involvement in the violence that goes on in Latin America, Iran, and Lebanon—violence done in the name of religion, or at least using religious loyalties as support systems. There are individuals, Niebuhr reminded us, who are educated to the point where they consider violence to be a form of savagery and superstition. They may believe that religious people are the source of all violence and that they themselves are enlightened and above such barbarity. (We have seen earlier that they fail to recognize their own religiousness at work.) These people are the intelligentsia, the educated elite, whose rational faculties have given them a sense of justice that has been refined by academic discipline. Some of these individuals are careful not to judge others harshly. They may be purged, says Niebuhr, of most egoistic elements and be capable of addressing the problems of human suffering.

However, Niebuhr reminds us that social groups and collectives are a different matter entirely. "In every human *group*," he writes, "there is less reason to guide and to check impulse, less capacity for self-transcendence, less ability to comprehend the needs of others and therefore more unrestrained egoism than the individuals, who compose the group, reveal in their personal relationships."

In other words, every social group or collective is something other than the sum of its parts. A corporation, a nation, a race, a religion (as institution or social group), an academic department has a personality its own. It is a form of power that is concerned with self-preservation and self-justification and will not be brought completely under the influence of reason or conscience. Many intellectuals fail to understand that the solution to our social problems is not simply a matter of getting individuals to give up outworn customs, "moth-eaten slogans and catchwords that do substitute duty for thought." Each of us is a self-interested individual. We may cover that self-interest over with theories and our own sense of enlightenment, but the self-interest remains; it becomes entrenched, predatory self-interest in our social groups.

The pilgrim knows this, simple and uneducated though he may be. "By the grace of God I am a Christian man, by my actions a sinner." And, dear pilgrim, you are a sinner based on the thoughts and actions of all the social groups of which you are part, the blood of which flows in your veins.

It is not only his individual action or inaction that makes the pilgrim "a sinner," but also the fact that he is simultaneously a member of numerous social groups. I may consider myself a pure and enlightened individual who rises above what I consider to be the outworn beliefs of Roman Catholicism with regard to birth control; but my salary comes from a state that is self-interestedly involved in those very nations where birth control is a problem and where the success of corporate industry depends upon exploitation of the poor. It would be better for me to confess with the pilgrim that I am a sinner in spite of my enlightenment. Perhaps then at least human understanding would be advanced.

As an individual I consider the religious violence in the former Yugoslavia, in Northern Ireland, India, and the Near East to be horrible, unenlightened actions, and I ask myself: "How is it possible? How can anyone conclude that his cause gives him the right to plant bombs, to take hostages, to blow up innocent people and set armies on fire?"

But I know that I am not so different from the terrorist. I know that I belong to a nation and to a grouping of nations that have exploited the lives and institutions of people in all those regions. I am a party to the violence of predatory social groups. Even my sciences and technologies are forms of exploitative self-interest that do violence to the lives and values of other societies—eroding their lands, uprooting their people.

There are no easy answers to any of the problems of human history. Much of the adventure of existence is derived from the inability to predict our own behavior at all times. Human beings are unfinished, indeterminate creatures. The uncertain future is a part of our existence. We can't be pinned down by anyone's definition or anyone's prescription for the good life—not even by our own definitions and prescriptions. The world's religious traditions, at their hearts, provide us with the wisdom to understand this observation and to make it a way of living effectively. They provide us with the means of being a pilgrim who knows that all people do bad things and are even responsible for bad things done by virtue of being an American, a Japanese, a South African, an Iranian, or a Sikh. People do bad things in the name of religion because human freedom makes bad actions possible.

Religions have the potential for teaching us the way of the disciple and the pilgrim; but they are also social groups, collectives that have the power to manipulate us to evil ends, to give expression to our predatory inclinations. Only the pilgrim knows what Martin Luther proclaimed—that we are all simultaneously saints and sinners. Always!

Why People Do Bad Things in the Name of Religion

Designed by Edd Rowell

Composition by Mercer University Press
    typeface—GillSans (titles), TimesNewRomanPS 11 (text)
    text prepared on LaserMaster 1000 printer

Cover Design by Lisa Kronholm

Production Specifications:
    text paper—60-pound White Acid Free
    cover—Arrestox cloth on standard boards
    dust jacket—100 pound enamel

Printing and binding by Braun-Brumfield
    Ann Arbor, Michigan